"And So It Is"

"And So It Is"

95 Lessons to Heal Your Soul and Transform Your Life —Loving Guidance from an Ethereal Voice

Carleen Chase

Cleveland Street Publishing

Copyright © 2022 by Carleen Chase

All rights reserved. No part of this publication may be reproduced, stored in a retrieval system, or transmitted in any form or by any means, electronic, mechanical, photocopying, recording, or otherwise, without the prior written permission of the copyright holder, except brief quotations used in a review.

Cover photo © iStock/magdasmith

Author photo by Joel Treadwell, Fine Portraiture

Interior illustration ©iStock/Deskcube

Design by Meadowlark Publishing Services

Published by Cleveland Street Publishing

Manufactured in the United States of America

ISBN 978-0-578-31907-0

Published 2022

"My words spring forth onto this paper to tell you and all:

I Am.
You Are.
We are One.
We are All One."

This book is lovingly dedicated to each person who seeks to release the old, limiting messaging, beliefs, and thought patterns that have imprinted on their souls—and to finally heal.

Contents

Acknowledgments...xi
Introduction xiii

Book One: Heal and Rise 1
Introduction to Book One: A Welcome from the Voice 3
1   A New Day................................. 7
2   How Do You View Yourself?..................... 17
3   Let Go—and Focus the Mind..................... 27
4   Turn Aside from Shadow 35
5   Learn to Navigate Change 45
6   Your Progress Is Visible......................... 57
7   Introducing "Real" 67
8   Find Peace and Renewal......................... 75

Book One, Part Two: Step Forward................. 91
Introduction to Part Two 93
9   Cleanse, Fill, and Receive 95
10 Go Forth.................................. 109
11 Live These Lessons......................... 121
12 Deepen Your Practice....................... 135
13 All Is Well................................. 149
A Closing Message to Book One from the Voice.......... 159

CONTENTS

**Book Two: Find Your Way Home—
Transform Yourself and the World**................. 163
Introduction to Book Two: A Message from the Voice 165
Author's Introduction to Book Two 169
14 "Home," the Temple of God, the River of Light,
    and the Light Beings 173
15 Living in the World 197
16 Come Within 213
17 The Energy of the All.......................... 229
18 Apply the Knowledge of the "All" 253
19 Three Essential Lessons 271
20 You Simply Know—You Simply Are 283
Closing Message from the Voice:
    And So It Is, and All Is Well 291

About the Author............................... 293

Acknowledgments

Without the love and support of many people, this book would not be possible.

It was my husband, Mark, who first encouraged me to craft these lessons into a book. He believed that they could help others as they had helped me. Not long after, the voice emphatically told me the same thing, and it was because of these messages that I decided to write this book.

My sister Cyndi, a successful author of several books herself, was the first to read the rough and unedited lessons. Her exuberant feedback was *"You so have a book!"* Thank you, Cyndi, for your encouragement and support.

My wonderful editors, Sheridan McCarthy and Stanton Nelson of Meadowlark Publishing Services, worked patiently with me through each iteration of this book, adeptly navigating between gentle guidance and stepping back as I worked to figure out my process. Their talent, strength, and editorial gifts (as well as who and how they are) enabled me to find my voice as a writer and actualize this book. Thank you for the many ways you helped and guided me through; this book would not be what it is without you.

Merry, my cousin and dear friend, filled me with unwavering support and love, and patiently read various drafts of the book encouraging and challenging me to go deeper and further. Thank you so much.

There are many amazing people who have supported me,

Acknowledgments

nurtured me, and lifted me up over the years. To each of you, I offer a sincere thank-you. Each of you has, in your own unique and special way, touched my soul and significantly impacted my life. Thank you for helping me grow, become a better version of myself, and source the courage to bring forth this book.

But back to my husband, Mark: You are my best friend, my love, my partner, and my co-walker along the path of life. I am beyond grateful that it is your hand I hold as I step through my day. Thank you for your help and guidance with this book … listening to (umpteen) passages from the book, knowing when I needed to wrestle through alone, and gently helping me along when needed. Thank you for the many evenings you cooked dinner (or got us takeout) when I was burned out from hours behind the computer screen. Mostly, thank you for being you and being my husband.

Zachary, my dear son: I am so grateful that when God gave me a child, He gave me you. Thank you for being who and what and how you are. I am beyond blessed to be your mom. And Winston: thank you for being my bonus son, for being you, and for all that we share in common.

Without the voice, there would be no book, and my life would not be what it is today. I am deeply humbled, profoundly grateful, and sometimes still in disbelief that I get to talk to and learn from you as I do. Thank you. So very, very much.

And finally, to each person who holds this book: Thank you for including me and the voice on your journey. May your path be bright.

Introduction

My journey is not yours, nor is your journey mine. But despite our nuanced life differences, we share many distinct commonalities: Our life paths are not always linear, nor are they always clear. The view is not always beautiful, nor are our days always brimming with sunshine. Our journeys wander and meander from moments of true bliss to what might feel like endless days of darkness—when we find ourselves residing too close to the abyss. All of us, undoubtedly, will traverse this wide spectrum of days throughout our lives.

During one of those days on my journey when I felt closer to the darkness than to the sunshine, I asked a question many of us ask from time to time: "How do I stop feeling this way?" Moments later something entirely unexpected and marvelous happened: I had the first of what would be many ongoing conversations with a wise, loving, and tender voice unseen.

The voice is that of a "teacher," a "guide," or a "sage" sent from the Creator—from the All, the I Am. He is the teacher and counselor I always longed for but could never find. He is *wisdom*, pure beauty, and Real truth. He is *profound love*, and since he first spoke to me in 2017, he has remained steadfastly by my side.

This "teacher," whom I call *the voice*, told me that these lessons—*this healing balm for our hurting world*—are to be shared. And so, this book is a compilation of many of the lessons I received from the voice over the course of about two years. As I now author these lessons into a book, I believe it is important for me to share that

Introduction

I am not the same person I was when he began to speak to me.

The voice and these lessons have changed me.

The lessons are simple, but they are powerful.

They did not come from me but *through* me, and the life-changing wisdom within them enables all of us to blossom into who we really are and the person we were always intended to be. With his tremendous love, and his ability to so simply and elegantly weave these timeless and universal truths into a process for living, this voice teaches us how to heal the wounds and the residual bruises we have carried as scars on our souls. He teaches us how to shed the negative messaging we have operated from, and how to quit reliving past traumas in our head. He teaches us how to navigate within—and through—difficult relationships, circumstances, and situations in the here and now. He teaches us how to step into—and live in—Real power and strength. And he enables us to stand grounded and whole, complete and full, that we might create a day of our own choosing, function at a higher frequency, and shine from within. *In short, he guides us to awaken into our Highest Selves by changing our minds and our perceptions of the world around us.* When we uplift our thoughts, he tells us, we uplift ourselves and our lives—and *it is then* that we have a chance to naturally influence and uplift the collective world around us.

If you are lonely, depressed, uneasy, remorseful, insecure, or stuck in the past; if you are worried about the future, trapped in your "story," uncertain of your own worth, or unable to stop dancing with your resentments—these lessons will teach you how to let go of the old and limiting messaging that hinders you from confidently and gracefully moving through life and creating each day of your own choosing. I am delighted to share these lessons with you, and I wish you well on your journey! Namaste.

My conversation with this voice unseen began one morning on my daily walk ...

Introduction

I was sad, empty, and ruminating on dark thoughts—again. Despite years of regular therapy and loads of self-help books and journaling, I found myself unable to maintain peace, emotional steadiness, and confidence within. Outwardly, I lived a successful life. Yet inwardly, I remained unable to stop myself from ricocheting back to what controlled me: my "story" about the things that had happened to me during my life and who I thought I was as a result. I ached to finally be free of the dark fingers of negative self-chatter that all too often reached up to pull me down. I longed for healing and transformation.

On this fateful morning as I walked, head down, watching one foot drift in front of the other, feeling bad (or more likely, pitiful), for some reason I recalled a silly-sounding conversation I'd had as a young child with my father. It became the topic of my first conversation with the voice, and as it turned out, this simple childhood memory laid the foundation for the lessons in this book.

In that moment, I was reminded that I'd asked my dad why I had inherited his big *dad* feet, while my sisters had my mom's feet (*girl* feet, I had described them, way back then).

My dad's answer seemed dismissive at the time, because he had missed the whole point of my young complaint. Yet despite the passage of many years, his insightful words had remained with me, and they now bubbled up to the surface, coming back to me clear as a bell—ringing a single, beautiful, resonant tone. "*You have my feet,*" he told me, "*so you will never blow over in a wind storm.*"

I smiled and looked up at the sky as I finally understood the wisdom that was always within my father's words. It was then, in that moment of clarity, that the voice emerged—speaking to me—and through me—in perfect personification of love, truth, beauty, and oneness.

The voice told me I needed to remember my dad's words. That

Introduction

I was allowing the winds of life to blow me wildly about, and that I was like a reed fluttering in every direction, untethered.

"Get into your feet," the voice said in his first message to me. "Ground yourself. Feel yourself consciously connected to the earth. Focus only on your feet, on being present in them, aware of each step, placing all your thought energy into your long feet. You are not grounded. You must get grounded. Focus only on this."

And so we began our discussion.

Morning after morning, we did this very simple exercise, this mind-shift work. It probably sounds like a small thing, but I was hungry for help, and this concept of *getting into my feet* proved to be the first of many positive steps I would take as the voice taught me how to unlearn (and release) thoughts and habits that no longer served me, and to design a wonderful life of my own choosing.

Various and many are the circumstances, situations, and experiences that define our view of ourselves, our perception of the world around us, and how we navigate our lives as a result. Some of these things, undoubtedly, will impact us more deeply and profoundly than others, and together they create a sort of operating system for how we unconsciously approach life. My "story"—aka my operating system—which I've needed to heal and release—began with the dysfunction of my family of origin, replete with neglect, abuse, and trauma.

I coped by escaping—as in, *get me outta here* levels of escape. When I was a child, though, there was of course no place for me to go. I was lucky to have had lots of small pets that I loved very much (birds, gerbils, a white rat, and hamsters), and a large rag doll named Mary that I took with me everywhere. I escaped into a make-believe reality with my animals and my doll, one in which we were all a family and we were happy together.

Escape was a reactive way of living and being that I would unconsciously continue for many, many years.

I studied classical voice, piano, and flute. These were easy and fulfilling distractions for me to get lost in, and I spent hours practicing each day, consumed by the beauty of the music. Although I became quite accomplished in all three, it took me years to comprehend that while I loved creating, expressing, and performing beautiful and moving sound, at its core my music was a form of escape.

In aerobics, the pounding music and constant movement stimulated wonderful mental and physical release—and I rarely missed an opportunity, often attending two classes per day. Looking back, I realize this was another dimension of escape.

Furthering the point, corporate America provided me with an identity of success, and I wrapped myself around my titles and achievements—these things reflecting back to me that I really was worthwhile after all.

Numbing my mind with large goblets of wine was no more helpful than any of the other escape options I had employed. And on top of that, it caused me to gain weight, so I felt even worse.

In short, nothing helped me move on from the pain I carried within. Not therapy, not books or journaling, not living in the coping mechanism of *get me outta here*. I remained unable to let go of my "story" and the feeling that I was somehow damaged and *less than* others.

And yet, there was always within me a tiny place of knowing belief—a spark of light that I could sense, that was always shining, even if quietly and dimly—telling me that I was worthy, that "it" would get better and I could have and would have a life of my own choosing.

The problem was, I didn't know how to get there.

❖

Introduction

And then I met the voice. This loving teacher, counselor, and ethereal guide gave me *hope* and a path out of the darkness. He told me that I could learn to create a life filled with peace, real strength, wholeness, and fullness, and that it was now *my* turn. That I could learn how to move beyond where I found myself, but I *had* to come back to my feet. He said that my father's analogy was exactly right, and not silly or flippant at all, that the conversation I'd had with my dad so many years ago had been fateful. That it was indeed my turn now—and my choice—but if I were going to change my life, *I must change how I think.* You cannot change your life, he said, if you do not change your mind.

So now we begin, he said.

Every day, begin it with me. Every day, lead off and set your day with me, and I will teach you and guide you.

And so he has.

Each morning I walk for about an hour with the voice, and when I get home he captures our talks on a broader level, through my pen and on paper. That is, when I walk with him, he speaks to me specifically, but when I write he usually speaks on a level applicable to all of us. Together we have captured his lessons and his loving words, and they compose this book.

Speaking in a familiar and fatherly manner, the voice talks to me, asks me questions, teaches me, and guides me. He has taught me to live grounded and firmly planted in my feet. He has taught me how to reprogram my mind from living in lack, shame, anxiety, self-doubt, and fear to living in wholeness, fullness, and completeness. Connected. One. Power-filled. Capable. Able to create a joyous day rather than continuing to live that day in the past or to be bound by the constraints of yesterday's belief systems. He has taught me that I am not the trauma I lived and have carried closely for so long: *that it no longer defines me.* That it is my time. I matter. I am never alone, and perhaps most importantly, I am deeply loved.

Inspiring words such as *dignity*, *truth*, and *beauty* would appear frequently in our later conversations, but the very first lesson the voice shared was practical:

Get in your feet.
If you are in your head, you cannot be in your feet.
Get out of your head.
Get in your feet.
Live from here.

This was the touchstone. We worked on this concept daily, and from there, when I was ready, he gave me each next lesson, encouraging me to heal, to rise, to step forward, and to not fall back.

To create myself anew each day.

Just as it is now my turn—it is now yours too. We need no longer define ourselves by what has happened in the past, or what happens in the here and now. We have choices! We are infinite, powerful, light-filled, radiant spirits having a human incarnation. We are loved, and we are never alone. And by learning, and awakening, and setting aside the messages of the past and the baggage we have carried for our lifetimes, we can step forward—confidently and brilliantly—on the illumined path that is meant for us.

About This Book

This book is organized into two parts—Book One and Book Two. In fact, I originally envisioned publishing them as two separate books, but I have chosen to put them together into one body of work, as the second book builds so nicely upon the first.

Throughout both parts of the book, the voice uses beautiful imagery, with much allusion to the concepts of *darkness and light*. These words may connote different meanings to each of us, and evoke different feelings as they are used. That's why before going any further, I think it is important to clarify the context of how the voice uses these two words. I believe he uses the word *darkness* to describe that which keeps us from being able to live from, and to express, our highest selves; darkness is those things that *cover* and *keep us down*, connected to our wounded selves rather than our higher selves.

When I think of how the voice uses the word *light*, I envision radiance, beauty, illumination, Real power, brilliance—the ethereal. *Love*. Angels are often associated with light. The *white light* is often used to describe the protection and healing of Jesus. In Eastern philosophy, light or enlightenment is the cornerstone of the process of becoming one's highest self. And in the natural world, light provides nutrients for growth. In her splendor, nature is often photographed with sunlight streaming down from heaven, peeking through foliage. By employing light—in the way the voice inspires—we learn to embrace ourselves as beings that are filled with light. And we are able to confidently step forward into the spectacular garden that is intended for us, deeply rooted and springing forth in radiant color for the remaining days of our journey.

But to do this, as with any journey, we must begin at the beginning: we must first heal our wounds from the past.

In Book One, the voice *comforts*. He reminds us that we matter, that we are not alone, that we are loved, and that the circumstances we find ourselves in need not define us—he helps us find relief and begin our healing. He provides a linear series of lessons to lead us from being who we *think* we are to knowing who we *really* are (a divine being having a human experience), so that we might *express our beautiful gifts, sharing our souls, our light*, and *our spectacular symphony* with all those we encounter.

He helps us awaken and shine.

He helps us get up out of the mud and radiate our brilliance.

We are each here at this time for a reason. We are here to awaken and to fulfill our soul's purpose. To do so, the voice teaches that we begin by taking charge of ourselves. He teaches that we are to no longer let the behaviors of others, the past, or the situations we are in today govern *who* or *what* or *how* we are!

I think of these lessons as yoga for the soul—they allow us to get hold of our mind and not allow it to control us. When we practice yoga regularly, our body is stretched and strengthened. In the same way, when we work these lessons daily, we learn to govern the runaway mind. Our soul becomes strong and filled, and we slowly blossom as does a beautiful flower, stretching to face the sunshine and becoming glorious in its presentation of its own simple yet beautiful splendor.

A special note about Book One: I do the Morning Exercise (Lesson 33) each morning to begin my day and my walk. Though it took some time for the voice to impart this exercise to me, I invite you to add this practice to your morning routine right away; you needn't wait until you get to Lesson 33 to begin. Further, after each chapter you'll find a "Notes" page. Taking time to reflect on the lessons, jotting down thoughts as to how they apply to your own life, will be valuable if you wish to witness your progress later, or as you go along.

The voice is cognizant that life happens, and that our minds can be tricky and sometimes sneaky. He understands that we may be going along just fine in our day, and then—*whammo!*—we're back to revisiting the painful and perhaps damaging parts of our past. Or we're auto responding to a stressful situation from our wounded, unhealed self, all because our mind decided to venture back into ruminating or because our unhealed self was triggered. In the lessons, the voice helps us recognize when this happens, acknowledge it, set it aside, and choose to go on.

So Book One is about deciding to get up: to rise, step forward, and not fall back.

I like that these lessons are about *how*—not just *what*. He teaches us these "yoga poses for the mind" so that we can become our true selves. We cannot become expert at yoga overnight; nor does

INTRODUCTION

becoming our highest selves happen overnight. It is a process—of healing, of growing, of blossoming each day. And in his simple way, he teaches us *how* to do it.

Book Two contains advanced lessons, esoteric in nature, that accelerate and deepen the teachings offered in Book One. Here, the voice presumes that we have become stronger and have moved beyond living in yesterday. He presumes that we are hungry and ready to understand the bigger picture.

In Book Two, he introduces us to the "temple within." He eloquently and vividly describes what this temple looks like and how we can access Real power through living in it, and through stepping into the energy of the All.

He uses metaphors and vivid imagery to enable and invite us to see the world around us in a new way, and he teaches us how to utilize this new way of seeing the world to uplift our energy and change ourselves.

He helps us employ universal truths to navigate the chaos and unrest that are occurring during a tumultuous time in our world.

He invites us to connect to the All, radiate our own brilliant light, and naturally become a catalyst to help others awaken and blossom as well. *In short, he inspires us to release the bindings of our mind and to fall gently into what is Real so we can brilliantly rise—like the Phoenix—into our grandest selves.*

A special note about how to use this book: I received these lessons over time—not all at once, or all in one day, and they read more like a collection of poems than a novel. So instead of sitting down and reading cover to cover, I recommend focusing on a single lesson each day, or if you are so inspired, perhaps even a chapter a day—small enough increments that you *absorb* the lessons so you can source their wisdom in any moment, as needed.

As you continue to revisit the lessons, in time you will find layers of meaning imbedded within each one. This, of course, is not reflective of a change in the text, but a change in *you*. Allow yourself the gift of realizing the depth of meaning woven into and through the words. Allow yourself the gift of living these lessons. They will provide comfort when needed, and further insights as you are ready, and as you progress they will deepen and solidify the shift in your thinking and perception of the world around you.

It is my time.
It is your time.
If not now, when?

Book One

Heal and Rise

Introduction to Book One: A Welcome from the Voice

And so it is ...

Welcome! Your journey awaits and your time has arrived. This is a new day: your day to shine, to step forward and to do so without fear. For within this forward step is your new life.

You must give up the past in order to grow into who you are meant to become. The past, the pain, the "story" you've clung to for so long, which you've used to identify yourself with and by, needs to fall behind—remaining as a color in your palette but fading in prominence on the canvas of your life.

As you grow and renew your concept of self, the gray, the shadows, and the comfort of the known must fall behind, serving as a reminder of who you once were and as a springboard to who you are becoming.

Each day, move in the direction of light and love. Each day, take a step forward and become one step closer to your Real self.

Do not blame others that your awakening has taken so long. Harbor no resentment. Step out of the known, your past, and your story and into the direction of your true self. You need not understand fully before taking the first—and then the ongoing—steps, for you are guided by the knowledge that comes from that place deep inside of you that resonates with your Higher Self and a higher way of being. Fear not and step away not. Your path is there—though perhaps obscured by your mind today. It will reveal itself slowly and surely as you strip away that which blinds you from seeing.

Your time is here. You are ready. Do not run from awakening. Do not lose perspective in order to fit into the norms of human living. You were brought here not to fit in but to bring forth your highest self. Step away from any thoughts that tell you to continue to conform.

Step away from any thoughts that you are not worthy; you are more worthy and loved and beautiful than you can even begin to comprehend.

Step away from any thoughts that you are not strong. You have weathered many storms and are courageous and growing in personal power: not power over others, but power filled and brimming with light, truth, and beauty, cleansed of darkness, remembering who you really are and stepping forward in confidence and dignity.

Step away from any thoughts that you are alone. You are part of the All, and one with All. You matter, and you have purpose. Believe not those messages you have heard from others who are still in pain themselves. You are worthy, and called to remember who you really are, and to live your life from this place where you know and remember that you are pure truth, beauty, love, and radiance. In you do I reside. Through you can I shine. As you walk through your day, consciously aware of being one with me, and as you allow yourself to heal and become who you are meant to be, you can forge a new life. One that is not defined by your past or the circumstances that surround you now.

Introduction to Book One

The path is easy when you get out of your own way and out of your mind. Cease the questioning, the doubts, and the need to know the route in advance, as this path is unlike others. There is no corporate ladder to climb. This is the yearning of the soul seeking to find its way to *Real*, to truth, to finding and expressing home, and to living as one while walking on earth.

Fear not. The circle isn't a roundabout leading nowhere! The circle is the connecting cycle of love energy and pure reality of which you are made. Allow it to be all around you. Allow it to fill you.

Live from this place today.

Live in the place in your mind where you know that nothing you see before you is Real, but that which *is* Real is inside, tapped into the reservoir of the most brilliant fountain of love. Light. Joy. Knowledge that is pure, not academic, knowledge that flows from the Universe to you. Your path is illumined. See it. Doubt not. Fear not. Question not. All is well. All is as it should be. You are opening as a flower, and as you grow you are able to share your light, truth, and beauty with others.

Not by preaching. Not with "better than," for all are one. Not in arrogance, for all are chosen. You are all here to bring your light and love to the corner of the neighborhood in which you reside. And in so doing, you will touch another's soul and light another's path.

Let the passages in this book resonate within you; they offer a pathway to healing. Do not critique their simplicity, but as you sit quietly with them, allow yourself to absorb the comfort, peace, and reminders of your worth and my love for you. As my lessons settle within your soul, may they heal and change you. The path to healing begins with

"And So It Is"

seeing yourself as worthy and then releasing your old story, stepping into light, and dealing differently with life, people, and situations in the here and now.

Life can be difficult. People will be people. Relationships aren't always easy. Not everyone is interested in healing themselves, and some people are not aware that they even have any healing to do! Therefore, interspersed are lessons about dealing with the ups and downs of relationships and of daily living.

Let the lessons unfold. Let them become part of you.

I see you.

I love you.

You matter, and you are worthy.

And so it is.

And all is well.

1

A New Day

Lesson 1: I Am with You

When I look back and remember *who I was* and *how I was* before I met the voice, I have tremendous compassion and care for the person I was then. As you now begin your own daily journey with the voice, I hope you too will one day look back on your first lesson with him and remember your former self with compassion.

I hope that his love, tenderness, wisdom, strength, and guidance touch you and transform you as they did me.

As you read the first lessons the voice shared with me, you will learn that he meets us where we are with acceptance and tenderness. He loves without judgment. He begins slowly and steadily. He does not expect us to have, nor does he offer us, immediate change. Instead, he first lays a strong foundation and then layers more levels of wisdom on top of the basics. He holds open the door of hope for us when he says, *"In time you will let these [the shadows] go, and you will stay in light."*

In today's lesson, we are reminded that we are never alone,

"And So It Is"

and that forces that we cannot see or understand are working in our favor.

Our job today is to accept ourselves where we are, release ourselves into the possibility of a better tomorrow, and allow ourselves to gently fall into peace.

And so it is ...
    By day and by night, by hour and moment,
    I am with you.
    I see how you respond to your past and the circumstances that surround you now.
    I hold you in light, that it will warm you and soften your edges.
    And still, shadows occupy your thoughts.
    In time you will let these go, and you will stay in light.

Lesson 2: Healing Is a Process

And so it is ...
    Healing is a process, my dear.
    It will hurt some, no doubt.
    But in the pain you will not bleed, but sustain.
    Sink into this moment.
    Be in this keener understanding and awareness.
    You fear much.
    Think on it less.
    Rest your worrisome mind.
    Give only tenderness to yourself.
    As you release, so shall you be filled.
    Dear one, rest now.
    Force answers not.
    Hurry healing not.
    I shall comfort you through.

In this lesson, we are given context for what we can anticipate on this daily journey: *Healing is a process ...*

Releasing the scars on our souls and becoming who we are intended to be: these do not happen in one day.

We grow a day at a time, day after day, taking one step after the other.

Growth is not immediate, and it will sometimes hurt. But in

"And So It Is"

this lesson we are beautifully reminded that *this too shall pass*. A better tomorrow awaits.

How lovely to know that.

When we are able to be inside the moment occurring in the here and now, purposefully and consciously—void of everything but what "is"—we are deeply, magnificently, and simply connected to that which is so much greater than us.

In these magical moments, we can know peace. In this place of pure truth and oneness, our minds can cease to run amok, and we can find the exhale.

Perhaps we are not yet where we wish to be, but in the *release* we allow ourselves to be filled. And by not forcing, we find our healing realized in its perfect time.

Lesson 3: Release the Shadow

Today the voice talks about setting down our troubles, a task easier to talk about than to accomplish. Many of us have longed to be free of the heavy baggage we have carried but have struggled with letting it go, and then *leaving it behind*.

The word picture the voice paints in this lesson helps us visualize releasing the darkness and baggage we have carried in order to finally be free of it. It also highlights the quiet peace and deep strength that will come when we are able to do this.

Making room for the gifts of light, peace, joy, and confidence is part of our journey, and as long as we remain filled with the shadow of the past, our vessels do not have room to carry the splendor that is intended for us.

And so it is ...
Give me all your fear, all your doubt, all your troubles.
Then, sit quietly.
As the darkness is released from you and washed away, you are left to breathe in quiet peace.
You fill with love. You are filled with light.
As shadow releases, you open to the gifts I give you so freely—to take in for your own healing and to share with others.
Darkness becomes light. Fear becomes peace. Joy

emerges. Anger diminishes. Sadness lessens. Doubt ceases. Cells grow. Confidence expands. Giving becomes natural.

Pause. Breathe. Open, open, open. Allow yourself to be filled. Allow yourself to receive. Ask for more from me. Allow my radiant light to flow down and around and permeate through and into all of your being so you are healed and we are one and all is well.

Push not.

Force not.

Let it come to you.

Let go and release gently anything not of this peace; you do not need to declare it done. Just watch the darkness flow away from you as dirt washes off your feet when you bathe. You pay the dirt no homage, no anger, no naming of that which it is. You only release it from its attachment to your physical body. So comes the release of darkness, anxiousness, fear, sadness, resentment, anger, self-doubt, shame, hatred: all those human, natural responses that are not productive for you.

So. Wash. Use my light and love to wash these away as the sediment that was once upon your feet, and as they go, wish them away in peaceful knowledge that they are gone.

And in that vacuum I can fill you with more light and more fully help you heal.

Lesson 4: Repel Darkness— Breathe in Peace

The voice speaks frequently about darkness and light—with the important point being how we navigate them. He teaches us that we can choose which of these polarities to reside in, and that we can choose which one to look at and focus upon.

In today's lesson, he says that *to ignore the darkness is folly, but to allow it into our being is foolish*. At no time does he encourage us—or teach us—to pretend that something dark is not there. Acknowledge it, he says. Do not pretend or ignore it—*just do not allow it into your being*.

We strive to stand so fully grounded in real strength and light that we become able to repel darkness and comprehend this truth: *Whatever swirls about us matters not*. This concept is easy to comprehend. It takes time and practice, however, for it to become a way of being and an automatic response. Here, we are inspired to acknowledge any darkness around us, get hold of the mind, and choose to not allow the darkness to permeate. If we do not allow it in, it cannot negatively impact our state of mind. Remembering this lesson—before we become triggered—is a powerful step we take in creating a day of our own choosing.

"And So It Is"

And so it is ...
Look not upon the darkness around you.
Let it enter you not; do not let it hurt your energy, your thoughts, and your soul.
To ignore it is folly.
To allow it into your being is foolish.
Acknowledge it and blow it away as you would the fluff on a dandelion.
It is not yours to have, to feel, to hold, to be surrounded and affected by.
Understand its existence and let it upon you not.
Stand tall and strong, and ground yourself in light, that any darkness around you is repelled.
Open yourself to receiving my continuous flow of love and light, and allow it to wash out all of the darkness that is in you.
Fear is darkness.
Unrest and doubt are darkness.
Breathe in peace.
Exhale all else.

Notes

2

How Do You View Yourself?

Lesson 5: You Matter

And so it is ...

It is not that you are undeserving, or that you are less worthy than others.

Those are the messages—unfounded and untrue—that were sent to you by people in pain themselves.

See the lack of truth within these messages you received.

You matter, and you are worthy *just as you are*.

You matter, and this day is an awakening for you.

See, know, and remember that you are worthy, strong, and more loved than you can even begin to comprehend.

Your life is blessed.

You have much to do.

You must not allow your fears and insecurities to mar the vision I have for you.

You see that vision and understand it in such a limited way.

Open your heart that you might see.

Release the messages of lack. Release the sadness.

"And So It Is"

> The past is over and no longer yours to carry.
> Quiet within.
> Peace, calm strength, and understanding are within you to claim.

❖

Today we are magnificently reminded that we matter, and that we are worthy just as we are. Part of the wonder of practicing these lessons is that we become able to comprehend these facts: We matter. We are worthy. We are strong, and we are loved. When we are able to finally stand firmly planted in this knowledge, we begin to see everything around us in a new way, and our life starts to flourish and blossom.

There is a flicker of another timeless truth in this lesson: *Healing ourselves is not about anyone else*. The voice notes that the people who (perhaps inadvertently) gave us the unfounded and untrue messages of our unworthiness were in pain themselves. I'm reminded of the phrase "Hurting people hurt other people."

In that truth, we are invited to forgive, and to let go of resentment and judgment—which are, of course, shadow thoughts harmful only to their carrier.

When we focus on other people (and replay negative and painful situations over and again in our mind), we cannot grow.

When we focus on realizing and accepting the truths that we too are worthy, strong, deserving, and loved, *we can grow.*

There are many entries in this book that help with this. We learn to see ourselves as the voice sees us, and how we really are. We see that we are divine beings, and that in our natural state, we are but light, love, truth, beauty, and real strength. That these qualities are ours to claim, if we will but choose more wisely. Learning that we need no longer be governed by the messages we received many years ago—from people who were in pain themselves—is both freeing and important.

Another layer within today's lesson is about fears and insecurities. In this lesson, the voice says: *You must not allow your fears and insecurities to mar the vision I have for you. You see that vision and understand it in such a limited way.*

Fear and insecurity are feelings many of us carry. They can show up in lots of different ways, or not much at all, but the fact that others may not see them in us or that we don't see them in others does not mean they aren't there.

I recently met a woman I experienced as solid, and grounded. She seemed confident, and she held herself with strength and poise. She was kind, and interesting, and our conversation was lively and fun.

I was surprised to learn later, from someone close to her, that she often feels insecure and inadequate. I was told that while she comes across as the woman I met, that is not her observation of herself.

Our sense of self has a direct impact on how high we will allow ourselves to rise.

The voice encourages us to grow beyond our fears and insecurities that limit us. It seems many of us do not see ourselves and our potential in the same way others do or the same way the voice does.

Look within at how you view yourself. Then, look deeper. Release any old belief that drives insecurity or tells you that you are unworthy. Release any sadness, any shadowy feelings, and step forward and away from this darkness. You have purpose and you matter. This is a new day. Believe the voice when he tells you this: You matter and you are worthy *just as you are*. He does not lie.

Today, stand firmly rooted in comprehension of your worth. From this place, step forward into your day confidently, purposefully, and deliberately.

Lesson 6: Decorate Your Soul

And so it is ...

You and I are one. There is no separation. As you sit, I am with you. As you move, the same. For connected is not enough to explain this; we truly are *one*.

Division is in your mind. I am one with all. You and I are one. When you forget this, when you move to aloneness, you cut off not only from human interaction but from the strength and solidarity of being one with All. One with the I Am.

Allow the merging of your human mind into the I Am. Allow me to fill your vessel with truth, love, light, and energy so that as you are, as you walk, as you go forth into your day, you know you do not walk alone. *You are not alone.*

My wish is that you would allow this truth to become real for you.

Carry nothing but these truths and all will be well. If it serves you not in lightness of being, strength of soul, direction of purpose, safety of movement, it is not of me and you must gently set it aside. It is not bad; it just serves you not. Your connection to that place deep inside of you that resonates with your Higher Self is yours to create.

See the tranquil water, the eye of the blue; hear the gentle sounds of the angels as they sing, and keep any thoughts of chaos, noise, anger, resentment, fear, and lack away.

How Do You View Yourself?

You are more than you have been told you are, and you are more than you have ever believed you are. Stay away from the messaging of yesterday: this is a new day. As you awaken you must shed the words that have been put upon your physical body and your cells, and rid yourself once and for all of the belief that you are unworthy and not meant for greatness. Your worth is astonishing, and your true purpose will present itself very soon. You must be strong. Your strength lies in the interior of your soul. Your strength is from your connection to the All, and that knowing place within. When you doubt, shadow is cast over this possibility. Let the shadow be not.

Let my colors spring forth onto the canvas of your being. Look within. You will not see darkness. And though your colors do not present in Technicolor, while they are yet pastel, they are pure, and their beauty shines. Allow this to be. Rush the process not. Do not allow darkness to muddy the picture I paint.

The time is here.

Leave behind the décor of your past. There is no room for fear, doubt, insecurity, and all other negatives.

Be purposeful in how you decorate your soul.

Your time has arrived.

We are each unique, yet we are beautifully and intricately connected. No matter what we do or where we go, we are one with the voice, the All, and everything that surrounds us. This is a wonderful reminder of what really matters: I am never alone. Nor are you.

Instead of thinking out of habit on any messages of lack, we are invited to merge our mind with these truths and the I Am, to allow our vessels to be filled and to carry only that which serves

"And So It Is"

us in lightness of being, strength of soul, direction of purpose, and safety of movement.

Pay attention. Be aware of your thoughts: What are you thinking about? If it is not about these things, let them go.

Today is a new day, and we each have a choice about how we will decorate it. Today, we are inspired to leave behind the décor of the past, and realize the color that now blooms inside us and around us. We are invited to bring that color forth into all we are and all we do—being purposeful in how we adorn our soul and our day.

What a lovely message to embrace today!

Lesson 7: Author Your Life

And so it is ...

Cease living the untruths you believe about yourself, and connect instead to the glory part of you that is Real.

All the rest is an illusion, a veil separating you from your potential, your light, and your joy.

When you step across the threshold from living the remnants of darkness into the creation of yourself today, all changes.

This is your journey, your challenge, your purpose, and your destiny.

When you shine despite your adversity, you can help others.

When you see that it is just a story, and that you are the author who is writing your story, you can, you truly can, write another chapter: one with a different plot and an entirely different ending.

And while you have always been the holder of the pen and the author of your life, you have not been ready to see and know that. They say that timing is most critical; had you awakened earlier, yes, you could have been writing your own script for all these years. But that was not your story.

You are now awakening. It is your turn now, and it is your time now.

"And So It Is"

So, you get to choose: Do you want to write your story so that you live in glory and radiance, or remain with the story where you live in shadow and darkness?

You need only be the playwright for one person: you.

Today, take along your pen. Draw your world, write your words, shape your form, and color it all brightly. Very brightly, my sweet dear.

For you are deserving.

And it is your turn.

I love you.

The voice encourages us, again today, to renew and uplift our belief system. He reminds us to *cease living the untruths we believe about ourselves, and connect instead to the glory part of ourselves that is Real.*

These twenty words are enough, on their own, to ponder all day—and for even longer. They remind us that *we are glory itself.* That the part of us that is *Real* is the part of us best described as *glory*.

I am, and you are—we are—all divine. We are all one. And we are all spiritual beings having a human experience. Today, cease living the untruths! Today, connect instead to the glorious part of you that is Real! Live from this place in your mind that knows you are so much more than you have ever believed you are, and live connected to the glorious part of you that shines!

When we become able to do that, the lesson deepens and expands—it becomes a call to awakening. Here, the voice lays the foundation for us to awaken to what our real journey is on earth—to step across the threshold from living the remnants of darkness into the creation of today. It is our journey, our challenge, our purpose, and our destiny. We are the creators of our day and of our reality. It begins by seeing ourselves—not as the untruths we have believed for a lifetime, but as progressing into awakening and writing a new, deliberate, and purposeful narrative for ourselves: one with a plotline and an ending of our own choosing. We hold the pen. We are the authors of our lives.

It is now our choice: Do we want to write the remainder of our story so that we live in glory and radiance, or remain with the story where we live in pain and darkness?

I know what I want.

Today, as you step forward into your day, choose wisely.

Notes

3

Let Go—and Focus the Mind

Lesson 8: You Cannot Make Sense of the Senseless

And so it is ...
    And so it goes.
    Round and round the crazy merry-go-round we whirl.
    You keep trying to make sense of the senseless. Order from chaos. Neat from untidy. And all around you is flailing.
    There is no tidiness where chaos is; where mess is, mess is.
    When crazy looms and you feel it inside, you must step away.
    Confusion muddies all waters.
    You cannot change what you cannot change.
    Let it go.

"And So It Is"

The voice beautifully connects his lessons to real life without judgment. He teaches us how to navigate day-to-day living and relationship ups and downs. It is very helpful to get close enough to these lessons that you can access a specific truth in your mind at just the right moment. I highly encourage you to revisit them frequently to reinforce them.

This lesson is one I think of when I start to overanalyze a situation and spin in my head, attempting to comprehend and then fix or control something or someone (neither the thing or the person, of course, being mine to fix or control). Now when I find myself doing this, I recall these words: *You keep trying to make tidy out of mess, and sense out of senseless … Let it go.*

This helps me find my feet again.

This helps me find my power again.

It is not always easy to interact with people, whether in short encounters with strangers or longer interactions with spouses, children, siblings, parents, colleagues, or friends. People are people. They have their own stuff. *We* have *our* own stuff. Confusion muddies all waters, the voice says.

This lesson teaches us to step out of the confusion, control what we can control (ourselves), and let the rest go.

The better we are at not stepping into other people's *stuff* and other people's triggers, the better our encounters and relationships will be.

The voice knows that this is easy to comprehend but difficult to execute. As the book progresses, we will find more lessons similar to this one—sometimes reminders are both helpful and necessary.

Lesson 9: Worry Not

And so it is ...

Welcome, my dear. I see you.

Take this moment and lean into the spirit I flow into you and all around you. Release into this rest and peace.

Worry not. Fear not. Let me be with you, and near you, and tell you many things.

You seek and I answer. You look and I am there. You grieve and I cry with you. You laugh and I light up in all things around you, for we are one. We are all one.

Let this be.

You are only beauty, only truth, only love, and become entangled with the mess of being human. Extract yourself from the tangles and be clean and free and one with me.

Trust me.

Trust in me. Do not go away from this peace.

When things appear confusing, stop, breathe, and look away from the confusion so that it does not get between us. In my reality, there exists no confusion. If you look away, pause, and redirect all your energy toward only what is Real, the confusion will melt away and all will be well.

Do not worry about the circumstances of your life. The details are merely things, and they are not worthy of your worry. The vision, the plan, and the life I envision for you exist far, far beyond the details you so wish to mess around in. They will strangle you if you let them. The life force

"And So It Is"

will turn dark, and then you will see me not and you will experience me not. Let only thoughts of my love and my lessons consume you.

I will give you thoughts. I will pave your way. You must walk the path, unencumbered by fear and uninvolved in drama.

Focus. Step wisely and confidently as you venture into your life.

Today, we are beautifully reminded that whatever we do, wherever we go, however we feel, whatever we see, we are not alone and we are not to be negatively impacted by the circumstances of what surrounds us.

The voice clearly tells us that *nothing is worthy of our worry*.

When our minds begin to run in circles, confusion is not far away.

When we stop the racing mind, breathe, and connect to what is Real, we naturally rise above the confusion and find peace.

Lesson 10: Focus on This Moment

Focus. Where is our focus?

What is it that we usually think about?

Other people? *Things* happening in our lives? Something someone said to us? Something someone did to us? Completing a detailed and full of analysis about *why* "they" did what they did, seeking to understand how a situation could have and might have turned out differently if only we had, or if only they had, done, or said something else? Pondering what we wish we had said instead of what we did say, or that we said nothing at all?

When our focus is on any version of these thoughts, we are not standing in our feet, nor are we grounded in strength. To realize peace, find the healing we seek, and live present in the here and now, *we must focus the mind*. And from here, when we are quiet and peaceful within, we will find ourselves naturally smiling into our life and our thoughts.

And so it is …
    Do not focus on others. For their lives are not yours.
    Focus on being present in this moment.
    Focus on my lessons.
    Listen to the quiet.
    Sink into these truths.
    Allow them to wash over you.

"And So It Is"

Let the healing continue. You are on a new trajectory. You are accelerating. The energy is fierce, and the time is now. You are arriving at your place of power. You are healing. No one can harm you.

Give no thought to those who wish you harm or exclusion; their energy will deplete you. Focus only on being grounded, in this moment, filled with light.

Give thoughts only to following my lessons, my will for you, your new direction.

Smile inside—you have a secret.

You are more than the sum of your parts. You are the I Am. The Alpha, the Omega, and you stretch wide and far, and your energy radiates all around you as love, light, joy, balance, detachment, success, peace, and all good things.

Smile into your life, into your thoughts, and let them express freely. If someone greets you with darkness, send it away—repel it so it does not even come near you.

Notes

4

Turn Aside from Shadow

Lesson 11: Step into the Light

And so it is …

Shadow surrounds within and without.

Look not into the shadow—instead step away and into the light.

The pollutant of another's darkness is competing for space in your spirit.

You must allow it to wash away, wash around you—not through you. That is all. Not within you. Do not allow it to permeate your cells. They are oscillating rapidly, not peacefully. They collide. They fire. They rest not. Allow them to settle as the bubbles slowly cease popping. Allow the emotion, the anger, the confusion, the craziness to merely bounce around you and enter you not. Think not of why. It matters not. Think not of how to respond. It matters not.

You are alone—but not.

For I am with you, and you are one with All.

"And So It Is"

Let the machinations go. Let the darkness stay in the shadows as you step away and into the light.

Life can be difficult, and it is easy to lose our feet.

In fact, it is easy to forget all about our feet.

A very important step on our journey to healing is learning to govern our mind so that we do not become triggered by what surrounds us.

Standing purposefully, consciously, and deliberately in our feet is important. Accepting that we can govern only ourselves is key. Remembering that we are never alone and that we are capable of choosing our response to any situation is a powerful step toward healing (and/or maintaining) our part of any relationship in the here and now. The voice is leading us to comprehend—at a behavioral level—that we are *not to react* to what is around us. The essence of this message is present in many, many lessons, repeated in different ways, to help us become able to transmute our automatic responses—reflecting both our intellectual acceptance of and the transformative nature of this truth.

Healing ourselves requires us to heal how we respond to people, places, and things in the here and now. We know we are healing when we no longer fall into retaliating with coping mechanisms, or lead with our hurt, wounded, triggered self. We learn to choose our own responses, regardless of any person or situation around us. In fact, the voice encourages us to be aware and grounded enough that we merely look away from shadow and choose instead to step into light.

If we remain in our feet, grounded, present, and alert, we are able to make these positive and healthy choices that the voice inspires.

Today, we continue to practice managing the mind. We can let the shadows in, respond to the crazy, and feel the same—or we can just let the "stuff" swirl about.

And not permeate.

It is our choice.

The world will go on around us as it will. People will continue to live their lives as they may. We strive to choose our responses, regardless of what surrounds us, at all times. Seeing through the eyes of our higher selves rather than our wounded selves enables us to choose wisely.

"And So It Is"

Lesson 12: Deepen and Expand

Today we embrace and celebrate progress. Yesterday's lesson was about choosing not to absorb and react to the shadows of others. Today the voice describes what success looks like.

And so it is...
Your arms stretch wider than they could yesterday. Stretching wider, you are capable of receiving more of all things, but ultimately, more of a release—and more of a *falling*—into the truths in these lessons.

As you grow, your spirit and your capacity expand.

You are deepening. You are becoming.

Your need for attachment is diminishing. And your need to control is dissipating—even your desire to control is fading.

Ruminating on the past, on other people, and on that which surrounds you is becoming unimportant to you.

You are evolving to let things be. You see other people's behavior and the situations around you as separate from you, and especially separate from your sense of well-being.

As you release these, you become more of yourself. As you release these, your peace, your sense of power, and your confidence expand.

Your need for others to do anything in a certain way or follow a certain formula ceases to matter to you. What others do or do not do bothers you not. What swirls around you bothers you not. You are not of these other things; let them go.

Cast your eyes, your heart, your love, your doubts, your fears on me, and allow me to fill you with strength and peace. In your contentment, let me fill you, and as you lean into me, gather the strength, love, and energy you need, that you might sit quietly and remain unaffected and undaunted by what surrounds you.

"And So It Is"

Lesson 13: Fill with Light and Strength

Today's lesson is the first in what will become an ongoing discussion about darkness on a broader and more global level. (Not all of the shadow we must heal from and manage comes from childhood, family systems, or the past.)

Shadow also presents wherever posturing occurs—world leaders and political figures come to mind—as well as through the media, the news, the workplace, interactions with those who are self-absorbed, and social media platforms.

The voice opens this lesson with the obvious: *Your people are experiencing their shadow side.* Sadly, it is not difficult to comprehend and envision frequent examples of this truth, but in becoming aware of the presence of shadow, we need not be unconsciously consumed by it. In fact, over time we will learn how to affect the shadows around us by changing our own energy. But I am getting ahead of the voice.

For today ...

Know that we each have the ability to *repel shadow* so it does not harm our thoughts, our minds, or our daily life. We each have the ability to be the light the world so urgently needs. We each have the power to drive away shadow—by refusing to be its carrier. When we are filled with light and strength, and able to stand consciously in our feet, there is no room inside us to absorb anything else.

And so it is …

Your people are experiencing their shadow side.

Darkness is powerful, but—hear this—not as powerful as light.

Be the light the world so needs.

Be in strength, calm strength, Real strength—in all moments, that the darkness cannot permeate you.

Light casts out darkness.

It doesn't mean darkness is not real.

What is happening is real.

Fall prey to it not.

Fall not into the fear it leaves behind.

You must gain in strength of light and love to overcome the shadow.

Lesson 14: Choose Where to Look

And so it is ...
  Cease to look upon darkness and shadow.
  It is but a distraction.
  It keeps you from what is Real, what is pure, what is true.
  When you cease to look upon this, it will fall away.

What we think about and focus on is a choice.

For many of us, choosing wisely is something that takes practice.

It is easy (and common) to ruminate: on others, the past, what is going on around us, worries about tomorrow—or even worries about what will come decades from today.

It has been said that *we can make of our life a heaven or a hell*. For years I pondered that statement, unable to comprehend its truth—thinking it highly unlikely for *people like me*. I mean, I had this childhood, you know ... I believed that my past was the reason for the way of my life—meaning that my inability to create my own heaven on earth was not of my own doing. It was because of ... (and the litany would begin in my head). It was inconceivable to me that I had the power within to simply cease to look upon it.

I truly wanted to live a life that was filled with peace, happiness, emotional steadiness, deep and meaningful relationships and connections, and healthy self-confidence. While I had moments and even stretches of time when I felt and lived in these ways, the ability to maintain these states eluded me.

Learning to live this lesson cannot be done by another for us, or learned by another and explained to us, or figured out and lived by another and then given to us. This is a step we each take—on our own—when we are ready, in our own perfect time. *All of a sudden, it just makes sense, and we recognize the shift in our thinking with deep humility and gratitude,* comprehending the power we have to make of our life a heaven—and nothing else—simply by changing our mind.

Notes

5

Learn to Navigate Change

Lesson 15: Release Outcomes

And so it is ...

To remain at peace when doubt flies about is the challenge. You are both up for it and prepared for it.

You will not be forsaken. Trust me.

Today. That is where you live. You plan, prepare, and work for tomorrow's needs, but live in the here and now. You are not lacking within today. Why should it be different tomorrow?

Come to me. Rest in my strength and know that I am one with you. As you carry yourself, so do I carry you. As you walk, so do I walk with you.

Fear not.

Quiet within, and connect to that which is Real and true.

Live as I inspire and instruct.

Let go of outcomes.

Fear not. I am with you.

"And So It Is"

There are times in life when doubt is present. We will each meet and experience doubt at some point on our journey, and we strive to keep it as a companion for as short a time as possible. During times of doubt, it is not uncommon to free-fall into the runaway mind, worrying about tomorrow, entertaining *what-if* scenarios. The voice encourages us to *focus the mind,* and stand firmly planted in the knowledge that everything will work out just right, for our highest good, in perfect time. Wise (and aware) is the person who learns to govern doubt. To do this, the voice encourages us to live in "today." We are to choose to be *here*: present, aware, and consciously stepping into all the possibility this day holds—not in our mind ruminating about what may or may not happen on another day that is not yet here.

In this lesson, the voice also encourages us to let go of *outcomes,* an interesting companion to doubt. When doubt is about, it is quite likely that we are worried about outcomes. What will be, when will it be, how will it come to happen, what happens if it doesn't happen, what if so-and-so doesn't do their part—what then? Any version of these inner questions means that doubt is present and we are worrying about outcome.

Learning to govern the runaway mind, and trusting that all will work out as it should, means *we must release outcomes.*

Throughout these lessons, the voice speaks repeatedly about what our most beneficial relationship with outcomes ought to be: we must leave them alone. They are not ours to work with, or to worry about, or to attempt to control. None of us knows what tomorrow holds, and more often than not the outcome tomorrow naturally brings is even more spectacular than the one we conceived of in our mind. Within the many sprinklings of this topic throughout both parts of the book, the voice remains clear: we are to leave outcomes alone.

We are to do our part, each day, day after day, as inspired, as we are able—as best we are able—stepping forward in deep confidence that everything will work out just right, as it will, when the time is just right. *When we bring our best selves to each day, outcomes will naturally solve themselves.*

Lesson 16: It Is Okay to Cry—But Do Not Wallow

And so it is ...

Do not be consumed by loss or change, or by the diversion of your life's path.

Rather, embrace the uncertainty you feel, and trust in me and in the process as I slowly unfold the petals of the flower that is your life.

You move from dandelion to elegant orchid, from weed to lotus. Your beauty resides in and around you, and I am with you.

Never fear, or think you are alone or that the walls of reality you've constructed around you are crumbling for no reason. I tear down the structures that are no longer useful in order to create the more magnificent and functional structures needed for today. The confines of the structures you call life—your life—are indeed coming down. Let them. Do not hang on in futility. Stand strong, in Real power and light, and allow me to help you rebuild what you have made, so it becomes even more magnificent.

You have much to do. I need you planted in place. I will make all things new. I will be the driving force in what and who you are becoming. Allow me to chisel where needed. Allow me to replant you in the fertile soil of the garden that is meant for you.

Fear not.

Trust me.
Trust in the process.
Come to me when you feel afraid.
Cry if you need to, but wallow not.
This is a good time. Good things are happening, and for you to bloom as I see you, pruning is necessary.

Elsewhere in this book, the voice describes our *journey to becoming* as an *ebb and flow*. It is not always an easy journey, nor do we always travel a straight line or straight trajectory to healing and becoming. We rise and sometimes fall down again. We step forward and sometimes fall back. Never do we berate ourselves for our humanness; this is just how "becoming" goes.

So goes the same in life.

Very few, if any, people set a course for life and achieve it while stepping forward at all times. There is an ebb and flow. And, as we know, it's in the ebb—those times in life when we are most challenged—when we grow the most. Perhaps we will lose a business during this lifetime. Perhaps a marriage, or a relationship that was important to us, or a job we liked well. Perhaps we are required to start over in a way we had never anticipated for ourselves. Whatever it is, we will each likely experience loss, or some type of significant change, during our journey on earth.

When the walls of life feel like they are crumbling, *let them*. Something new will come. The loss—and not knowing what tomorrow will bring—may hurt, and even ache, but the voice assures us that we will comprehend the pruning at a later time. We are told to not allow ourselves to fall into fear but to trust the process, stay in our feet, and keep going. *We are allowed to cry, but not to wallow.* Emotions might spill over—then we regroup and get on with it again. We dry our tears, rise up out of the mud, clean ourselves

"And So It Is"

off, straighten our spine, get into our feet, and step forward. We keep going, no matter what, because if we do not grow through our time in the mud, we will not realize the blossom of the beautiful lotus flower.

Lesson 17: Focus Your Gaze

And so it is ...

You have had much to see and to face. You have done well.

You walk with peace and confidence and love, and not with shadows.

Look not upon the outer perimeter of your path where shadows sometimes appear.

Keep your eyes focused straight ahead. Keep your gaze set on peace, light, love, and calm strength. On those things that are clean, not those that confuse.

When the confusion, the muddy, the achy, the fearful present upon you, you are to look upon them not.

Immediately brush these away and re-center on what is pure, true, clean, clear, and not of darkness.

Throughout this book, we find many reminders related to the same topic: focusing our mind.

The voice is cognizant of what it requires to create change at a fundamental level. What we think about, look at, and focus upon—and the ensuing internal dialogue that rattles around in our heads—have, over time, become habitual. *And to change at a fundamental level, we must change our mind.*

We do not read or hear a "truth" just once and accept it, live

"And So It Is"

by it, and be forever changed by it. It is one thing to comprehend something (and even to agree in concept) and another thing entirely to be able to shift our thinking to be in alignment with that new truth as an automatic reflex. This sort of change takes time, practice, repetition, getting it wrong, getting it better, trying again, over and over and over again, until finally we are able to create a new habit. A new way of being. A new way of thinking.

The voice deliberately restates his lessons in many different ways over the course of many lessons so that as we continue to practice, we slowly, and over time, *become*. Change of the psyche does not happen overnight with a magical *poof!* In the same way, when we begin a yoga practice or an exercise regime, we dedicate ourselves to working with the principles on a daily basis. We can then grow stronger and more flexible—over time. We learn to not push beyond where we are on any given day, and to work with the body we bring to the exercise mat on that day.

Today, we are told upfront that we have done well—we have strengthened our soul. Yay, progress is visible! We walk with more peace and love and with less shadow. We are then reminded to continue. To keep ourselves and our mind focused on our path, our gaze set on what matters, stepping forward, one foot in front of the other.

The voice knows that confusion and muddy, achy, and even fearful feelings will present themselves again.

We are gently reminded how to manage: brush the shadow away, re-center on what is Real, and keep going.

Lesson 18: You Have Much to Bring

And so it is …

Today is your day. I am with you. I protect you and love you, teach you and hold you. I hold the base of you in my hands as you walk into and through your day. You have much coming. You have weathered many storms. Rest. Relax. Sit with me in quiet meditation, that I might pass more light into your being, for strength and for chasing out all that is harmful for you and to you.

Yes. You are tired. Lean on me. Lean into me. Let me wash away the emotions and those things that are no longer related to your growth.

You have come far.

Fear not.

Look upon yesterday not.

This is your moment.

Walk with me. Walk in light, and be so filled that darkness hides its face, ashamed of coming near you and trying to harm you. The darkness is leaving you. Let it slide away into the night. You are not required to see it leave. Trust that the power within you is sending it away, scared and slithering. Your time of darkness is over.

Your wholeness is becoming complete.

Let this unfold as I have seen for you. You must rest and gain strength. You have much to do and to bring.

"And So It Is"

❖

We are never alone. We are protected and loved. We are cocooned in light.

Today, carry this message with you through the day, in all the moments when you are able.

Today, don't look upon yesterday—leave it where it is.

This is your moment.

Your time of darkness is over: Your wholeness is becoming complete.

Your future is beginning to unfold.

Hold these thoughts close today.

Hold the last sentence in today's lesson close to you too—it is an important reminder. *Only you can bring forward your unique gifts.* Release the shadow within, and recognize who you are intended to be. Share your soul, your light, and your spectacular symphony with all you encounter. Step forward, deeply rooted in confidence and inner strength—and fulfill your destiny.

You have yet to realize the swell of the music and the vividness of the colors within you.

Keep going.

You have much to do and to bring forth.

Notes

6

Your Progress Is Visible

Lesson 19: You Are Awakening

And so it is ...

Embrace this new day, this new life, this new way of living your life.

Gone are the days of darkness, worry, fear, self-doubt, sadness, anger, and judgment.

The path for your feet to tread is new and fresh. I have made it so.

Gone is the emptiness, the shell of your being.

Instead you overflow with light, joy, energy, love, and the desire to bring, share, and connect.

You are awakening and living in a new way. Those desolate days were purpose filled but they are now over.

Now you can look back and compare your days of then and now. Never again need you fall into the cave, the dark, the abyss, the nothing, for all of that is replaced and filled, and no more is your vessel a cavity. Now your vessel is one of nourishment, so that all of you may flourish and shine.

Let this be. Let this happen. Do not rush it or force it.

"And So It Is"

Do not analyze or think too much on it. It is yours. It is indeed unfolding, much like a flower whose petals stretch to face the sunshine and bloom, gleaming in bountiful color and filled with fragrance, so lovely yet so gentle. To embrace this unfolding and take it in is to find your own sense of clean and your own beauty to behold. Let this happen.

Look upon it. Love it. Take it in and relish its beauty, for you have waited many, many years and thousands of days for it to come together and for the wholeness of your being to unite.

You are one with me, with all of time, with that which is—simply because it is—and in this space, in these moments of recognition of the I Am, you are Real and full and capable. Not of your own accord but because of and in spite of yourself.

You are slowly shedding the false self and stepping into oneness with All. You are finding your Real identity, not as the world sees it or you but as who you really are. There is nothing else. Nothing else exists. Fear not. The shedding is purposeful. Trust in me. Trust in the process. Do not ponder it too much. As you connect within to that which is Real and true—as you access and speak with your Higher Self—you are touching the Divine.

Forget not the sisterhood and brotherhood. Step into the circle, join hands, and sing along with their angelic voices. Look not upon the details of the past or the darkness of yesterday. Let it pass. Let your light shine. Shadow is smothered by light. Keep your eyes focused on the light so that when darkness appears, it cannot pull you in. Look upon it not. Reside in it never again.

Live in this place with me, and with those souls who have gone before you.

You need to gain more strength. Find time in your day

to exercise, to build up stamina and vigor. Take care of your vessel, so that as it fills with power, it will not crack and will instead radiate that which is within.

Your time is here.

Yes, our time is here! The voice says this repeatedly throughout the book, partly because it truly is our time, and partly to help us remember why we do this work. It *is* time! If not now, when?

Wherever you may find yourself today, the voice places hope on the buffet table: we can have this new life, and this new way of living in our lives, if we will but receive.

Gone, he says, are the days of darkness. The path for our feet to tread is new and fresh. Take the step forward on this path!

Gone, he says, is the emptiness within. Instead, we overflow with blessings. We can see a new life. In truth, we can claim a new life.

We are now far enough along that we can compare yesterday to today. We have now grown enough that we can remember being pruned (we might have cried, but we did not wallow), and we are beginning to flourish and shine—maybe not all day, every day but more often and for longer than before.

We are to let this happen. We are to continue to step forward, and to not overanalyze or get wrapped up in confusion through trying to comprehend. We are to live inside this moment, knowing that while there is more to come, today is better than yesterday.

We are one with all that is, has been, and ever will be. We are one only with beauty, and when we are able to stand in this place, filled by connecting to that which is so much greater than we are on our own, we grow, we become, and we finally shed the false self. We can then step into who we really are—connected and able to enter the ethereal circle of the sisterhood and brotherhood, joining

"And So It Is"

hands with the angel souls who have gone before us and are now protecting and guiding us.

Stay here, the voice says! Remain connected to the beautiful and pure sound of their holy voices. Breathe in and breathe out—from here. We are to approach our day from this place of groundedness and connectedness.

And when darkness reappears, we allow ourselves only to skim the edge of its arc with a fingertip, that we will remain aware of its presence but do not allow it to burn us or draw us away from this beautiful place.

Lesson 20: Healing Progresses— Darkness Recedes

And so it is ...

Smile! It is a new day. You bring to it renewed eyes and a fresh perspective. Your healing progresses, and the darkness recedes. The light of all things shines forth and cuts through the shadows. Look upon this day and all things with the knowledge that today is good, today is fresh, and today the darkness diminishes, allowing you—the freed bird—to fly.

Look back not. The past matters not.

The days of sorrow, sadness, bewilderment, confusion, chaos, and lack of order are gone.

Step confidently into the direction of your day and your life, for I am with you and around you, supporting you, carrying you when needed—and shining always.

Fear not.

Breathe and know that you and I are one. We are all one.

You are safe. And you are. And you shall always be. In purest form, brightest light, warmest sunshine.

Bask in that knowledge and fear not.

And rest.

"And So It Is"

We stand fully grounded in this day, not wandering to the past or jumping in worry to tomorrow. We release the worn out and shadowy messages we have (perhaps unconsciously) carried within.

Carry this new messaging with you today. Let your growing strength and light prevail.

You really are a freed bird.

Fly.

Lesson 21: Your Day Is Shining!

And so it is ...

Your day is shining! Your spirit is alive and dancing. Your time of awakening is speeding along. Let it happen. It is not work. Just be it and do it and let it unfold before you and within you. Fear not, and let things occur as they may and will. Your light is bright. Your vessel is gaining strength. As you spend less time in the chatter of your mind and more time focusing on your foundation, on drawing strength and power and life force from the earth—the universe—the chatter dissipates and your power manifests real strength, real change, real ability to become one. Your merger has begun. You will draw power from beneath you as you walk, the well of divine nature and force drawing up into your human flesh and filling your cells as no other source can do. It is Real power. Real life force—life itself that flows through you. As this power increases, you quiet, and find little need for distraction—for that which is not Real. The distractions are leaving you, and you can prevent the mind from taking you back to them by moving from your head to your feet. From blindness to realness. From empty chatter to wholeness.

This is happening.

You are in motion.

"And So It Is"

Today, the voice points out many of the ways we have grown and blossomed.

Reread the lesson above and savor its splendor.

If only we could begin each day with the conviction of this lesson's first thoughts: *Your day is shining and your spirit is alive and dancing!* In perfect time, we will begin each day as such.

Notes

7

Introducing "Real"

Lesson 22: Behind the Material Realm

And so it is ...

Throughout the ages, it is fear that blocks all.

When you lean into it, it goes.

When you allow it to flow, it comes. Hence, the lesson of all things.

Chase not. Fear not.

Your world is not as you think it is.

That which is Real is what exists behind the material realm: the energy of all things. What you see is but a reflection—a mirage—a temporal experience of Real. Man chases what appears to matter, but nothing Real.

This lesson is one to read, reread, and ponder—to come back to again and again.

"And So It Is"

In fact, it is so important that the voice brings the last section of it up again, word for word, in Book Two.

The voice has placed each lesson in order. He often "seeds" ideas and then comes back in later lessons to fertilize and water the lessons, repeating them either in their original words exactly or in a new way, that the truth might germinate further. Again, the voice knows that we will not change the way we think by merely reading a lesson once.

He thrives in the simple. He teaches in the repetition.

There is nothing I can add to this lesson that will allow its depth to spring forth.

The layers of meaning embedded in this lesson—and in all of the lessons—will continue to reveal more depth of meaning to each of us, as we become able to see.

Lesson 23: Hold the Energy of All

And so it is ...

We step aside from ego to join the great circle of the I Am, the energy connector and life source. As you breathe and rest into this space of peace and expansiveness, I arrive.

My words spring forth onto this paper to tell you and all that I Am. You are. And we are one. We are all one.

When you separate, you pull away from the life force connecting you to the whole, to the Source of all things.

It is within this whole, *this place*, that all possibility and all that is Real exist. You create from here. When you are in this mode, you can hold energy between your hands like a ball. You can toss this energy ball back and forth, stretching it into material form.

If it is peace you desire, intend peace into the ball of energy between your hands. See it and feel it.

If it is love you desire, intend love.

If it is abundance, intend that abundance and allow it to wash over you.

I Am.

I Am here to give.

You need only hook up. Hold my gifts.

Hold and stretch and intend the energy of All that is between your hands, and all things you intend shall come to you—if you will but receive.

"And So It Is"

❖

This is another lesson that will grow in depth of meaning over time.

We will learn it and become able to *experience* its truth, not only comprehend it. In fact, this lesson is another one "seeding" upcoming lessons contained in Book Two.

The voice is slowly walking us to a threshold of a new way of viewing the world around us—and then leading us through the door that separates the physical dimension from the energy realm of what is Real and true.

For today, allow the lesson to wash over you—that you can fall into the wholeness, completeness, and fullness it evokes.

We will come to know that within this whole, this place, all possibility and all that is Real, pure, and true exist.

We will come to know that we can touch this place and reside here.

For today, it is enough to know that it is here and available.

Soon we will understand it and experience it with greater awareness and awe.

Lesson 24: Radiate Light

And so it is ...

Your power is consolidating. Your light is brighter. Your energy emanates and flows from the core of the earth to the edge of the planetoids. You are now expressively part of the cosmos, of the great I Am, able to freely fly and navigate through time and space. And in that expression, to be and feel and show Real love.

When you speak, allow me to flow through you.

Be conscious. Be aware. Feel this energy.

Source me.

Source the great well of power I offer that requires absolute removal of self and ego.

Let me be your beauty. I Am.

Let me be your joy. You are.

Let me be your abundance. You have.

Let me mask and cover all fear—it is not Real.

Let me be within you and through you and of you, so that all you are is spirit force. But when fear or doubt reappear, acknowledge their return and focus instead on being filled with Real power and light, so that you will share only that which matters—true love, true acceptance, true knowledge that all is well.

Your time is near. You are stepping into your gift. You are expressing differently now, intuiting as I would have you do. You must not fear. You must stand firm in the light

"And So It Is"

that shines down upon your head so you can radiate light.

Fear not. You will not be lost. You are becoming of a higher nature, and as such you can help uplift the energy on your planet. Change happens when you change yourself.

Look not to your neighbor, your spouse, your family, the news, or anything or anyone else to change. Just quietly and simply live from this place. Focus not on outcome. Focus on this moment, this truth, this time of the here and now, and shine. In that beacon of light you bring, all around you is changed. Do not worry that you are too small, too insignificant, in contact with too few people during a day. Do this now. Live in this light. The outcome is not yours to control. Your job is only to live as I show, as I inspire, as I instruct.

Change happens in the mundane; this is where it happens.

Joy springs forth.

Peace settles in.

Light shines forth.

Darkness is shut down, gently—but powerfully—and fear dissipates, as a shadow crawling under the floorboards, never to be seen again.

It is on this day that light happens. It is in this moment that darkness is erased. Love. Not freely sexually. Instead *Be Love*. Walk in it. Carry it and let it flow from you. It is so large within you; you cannot contain it in a vessel of your size. It streams out of you.

Put on your cloak today.

Straighten your crown.

Radiate and carry this flow of light just as you are as you go through your day. Only light exists—that is what you are.

❖

There is so much wisdom and wonder in this lesson. Each time I read it, I find my soul naturally becoming one with pure, quiet beauty and truth—as if it has been inspired to awaken further. Perhaps it will come to kindle the same things in you.

Notes

8

Find Peace and Renewal

Lesson 25: When Choosing, Seek Peace

And so it is ...

See not the troubles around you.

But neither deny them. Instead, focus on that which does not upset you.

Nothing is changed by the fixation of thought.

Rest easy, in the calm expanse of my love. Lean in. Close your eyes and think not of those negative things that hang like low fruit. Leave them for another to pick.

Your day is worth more than that. When choosing, seek peace. Leave the drama train to go on its way, lickety-split, and quiet your mind in my peace. I bring no drama.

In truth, in that which is Real, there exists no confusion. Do not seek to see confusion. Let it wash by you so quickly that it is as though it is not there at all.

The slowing of your heart begins.

The negative feelings fall away.

Darkness lifts and light enters your realm today so you can reside in peace, light, strength, and Real power.

"And So It Is"

Here we are again ... another lesson to help us deal with people, places, and things.

It is the same message he has shared before, but expressed in new words. Obviously, this is a critical lesson.

The voice knows that to grow and change and become who we really are and who we are intended to be, we must become aware of where we are placing our focus, and master what we choose to think about.

Are there troubles around? Certainly. Do not pretend they are not there, the voice says, but do not ruminate.

Nothing, he says, *is changed by the fixation of thought*. How true that is.

We have a choice—the voice tells us to *choose peace*.

Today, that is our goal.

Do not think on negatives. Let the drama train go on its way, lickety-split, without you.

I find that when this proves difficult, a simple mind-shift tool is helpful: I tell myself that tomorrow I can choose differently. *Tomorrow*, I tell myself, *I can think on the negatives, and even climb aboard the drama train. But not today. Today, I choose to let it go.*

Or—if need be—when the mind and desire are very strong, I tell myself that in the next hour, or even in the next five minutes, I can choose differently.

But not now.

To heal, grow, awaken, and become our highest selves, we govern the mind. The voice told us upfront that to change our lives, we must change our minds. This is another example of learning to do just that.

There is great power in choosing wisely.

Lesson 26: Let Go of Anxiety

And so it is ...
    Confusion and noise surround you.
    Let those who wish harm, who desire chaos, who bring unrest fall away from your attention. *When you see them not, they affect you not.*
    You have much to do. But your anxiousness is palpable.
    Let it go and I will iron the creases of your emotions into smooth satin, so your heart, stomach, head, liver, arms, torso, legs, and feet are free of the stressors brought on by angst.
    Calm yourself and rest in me. Let me soothe you and protect you.
    You must find peace.
    The world is noisy and distracting.
    Come unto me.

There will be days like this.
    There will be days when the world around us is noisy and distracting.
    There will be days when people in our lives are difficult to get along with. People who wish us harm, or who have wished us that in the past. People who desire chaos. People who bring unrest to us.

"And So It Is"

This lesson reminds us that we cannot change what we cannot change.

But we absolutely can change what we focus on.

We can choose to let go. We can choose to stop trying to fix anything or anybody.

The image of our anxious emotions being ironed into smooth satin is another technique the voice gives us to manage the mind. It is easy to envision the satin and sense our fingers gently touching the soft, shiny fabric. Visualizing this can evoke a feeling of calm and offers the ability to focus on beauty and on what we can control instead of the drama spinning crazily around. We become able to put the situation out of our head and set it down. We become able to let it go. We can remain focused instead on the beautiful image of our emotions being ironed into smooth and soft and cool and lovely satin—feeling much better.

And then, to further explain, another lesson follows … with even more beautiful imagery.

Lesson 27: Fall Gently onto the Canvas of the I Am

And so it is …

There.

You quieted.

You're calmer.

Your heart beats more slowly, and in tune with the rhythm of the angels. Let their chorus and their peace come unto you as you carry them throughout your day. They magnify everything you are, and what you see, and how you are.

Let their light and their radiance envelop you as you walk through each step of each day. Your path is sacred and bathed in light. Be deliberate as you place your feet.

You must not fear.

Think not about tomorrow.

Think not of what your life is becoming—for it matters not.

We are quickening, and the readying is all around you. Lean into me. Draw strength from me as you walk. Do not deplete. Remain connected to me and to the great source of all things and to the I Am. Be one with the All of the All. The universe is small. It can be held in a tiny droplet shining brightly as it falls gently from heaven. The universe also surrounds every place you imagine you can be or go.

"And So It Is"

As you breathe, as you rest, as you exhale, as you release, you are falling gently onto the canvas of the great I Am, where all possibility is open to the creation of your mind, heart, and soul.

Fear not. Do not think too hard with your mind, but instead let me wash over you and carry you to this place where all that is, is the I Am: where you are reconnected to the whole, and filled so completely that no anxiety, no person, no "thing" can separate you from this divine love.

You are this love.

When you feel you cannot be this love, when you seek revenge, when you get angry or anxious inside, turn inward. Turn to me, and rather than see another in your mind, simply place yourself back in the hollow of my cradle. Let me hold you and caress you and rock you and remind you of who you are and let you find yourself again.

Lesson 28: Step Forth in Faith and Love

And so it is ...

Await not. Step forward into your new life now. Step in faith, in love, with purpose so that all you see, say, touch, share, and experience reflects only light and love. As you detach from that—as your thoughts wander to yesterday's woes, yesterday's pains, today's fears—you lose the ever-loving touch of peace, acceptance, and joy that gives you the ability to transcend your human endeavors and become more like me. *Focus.* See light, not darkness. Bring love, not revenge.

For when you look upon your neighbor, you look upon me and you look upon the All. Don't let their shadows manifest in you. Don't let the errors of their decisions become united with your own intention, for that is the darkness encroaching upon your own purpose, and it means the loss of your significant gift.

This is why I say to you: Look not upon the darkness. Feel not the sadness that still resides within. Let darkness and pain melt and then wash away so they cannot meld into your spirit.

Rest.

Get stronger.

Fear not.

Love one another.

"And So It Is"

Overlook those who wish you to live in shadow. Do not ignore them; look past them, beyond them.

You must cleanse within. Rest. And in your rest, fully let them go. Watch the residual sediment of their behavior fall aside and away.

And when you are free of the grime, you will be clean. You will shine brightly. You will feel warm. You will share love and express glory. You will exude joy.

Nothing, no one, no "thing" can harm you but your thoughts. You want to change your life, change your experience of the days? Then let go of the past. Quit ruminating on others and look to the light, to the Source, to the Creator of all things.

Allow me to breathe life into your dreams and visions.

All is possible.

All is creatable.

All is yours because you are a part of the Divine.

Truth indeed.

Lesson 29: Here, All Is Well

And so it is …

We begin another day together through fresh eyes and with a clear heart.

Let me speak to you, to fill you with knowledge of my love for you, and of the power you can access through me and through my lessons. Too often you remain alone and disconnected. Too often you go alone. Hook up.

Link to me, that all thoughts, all actions, all steps you take are one with me and we are connected as a river of energy that flows from me into you and over and around you.

Fear not. No harm can come between you and this moving force of living light and love. No danger can enter the Divine protection and physical manifestation of my embodiment that is all around you. And when you sync your mind to the ethereal, when you place your thoughts upon what is Real, you will see the greatest change in the days of your life.

As you walk, I am there on the path, beneath you, emanating love, peace, confidence, protection, up into and through you.

As you are, I am there above you, shining light upon you and into you.

In your day, you receive my presence from above and below.

Feel it. Know it. Bathe and lather in it.

"And So It Is"

>   I give it to you to bring peace on this earth.
>   Inside this place, all is well. All is safe. All is possible.

We are never alone.

How lovely to know and to be able to envision what it looks like—divine presence all around. Inside this cocoon of love, light, and protection, we are safe.

Lesson 30: Let Light Be Your Shield

And so it is ...

Fear not.

Cower not.

Stand strong in your feet, straighten your spine, chin up and eyes up.

Stand grounded in my strength and fluid in my love.

Expressively radiate light, and do not allow the darkness you encounter in others to shut you down.

Let your light be a shield of protection. That darkness enters you not and becomes of you not. Instead, project your light ahead of you, as a warrior sends his troops ahead.

My weaponry, my tools for protection, are light and love—and they hurt not.

They are there for self-protection against the darkness you encounter. They are a field of energy that can be absorbed by those you meet if they so choose, thus changing others as well.

When we stand straight, in our feet, shoulders back, chin up, eyes up, aware of being inside the moment, and firmly planted on the path beneath us, grounded in strength, we are whole. We feel complete and full. We have no room inside us for fear, self-recrimination, doubt, second-guessing, or shame. We can understand at the deepest

"And So It Is"

level what the voice says: *I am. You are. We are one. We are all one.*

When we are in this place of wholeness and fullness, what happens around us, and what other people do or do not do, no longer controls us. *We just are.* We step forward with peace and calm strength within.

Our best weapon against darkness is to connect and fill, to be protected and shielded by a field of light energy that no darkness can permeate. I remember receiving this lesson about weaponry. The voice said, "My weaponry, my tools for protection, are light and love—and they hurt not." It was such an explicit image. I could see soldiers on a battlefield wearing breastplates, kneepads, headpieces, shields, and swords—the outfitting we have seen in many movies. But to see weaponry as light and love conjures a very different image. Think of it: protecting oneself does not require the wearing of fighting regalia in the traditional sense, but instead requires fortifying with light and love. In doing this, the voice says, we are not only divinely protected, but we leave behind a little light and love—that those we meet along the way might be uplifted rather than harmed.

Lesson 31: Give from the Source

And so it is …

Give not of your entity, of your essence, of your sacred space. Give of me.

Give my overflowing, abundant, and ever-replenishing, eternal, omni-giving light such that you are not depleted but instead channel my light and energy.

When you give from your own energy, you deplete.

When you give of me, you are refilled continuously and abundantly. And at the time of giving, your cells expand in their capacity to hold more of me and more light and love.

As you expand, as your vessel becomes stronger, the I Am grows in you, and the eyes you use to see, the face you call your own, the skin that breathes the environment in and out become more and more of me and more angelic.

You are becoming and melding with the ethereal.

Soon your presence, not the words you use, will announce your peace and tranquility.

Soon you will be even more light. And yet more.

You give of me and I give you more.

I fill your vessel all day long as water from the faucet. Question it not. Let this circle of giving and receiving happen through you and of you.

"And So It Is"

Today, give from the Source,
        and allow yourself to be refilled,
        all day long,
        as water from the faucet.

Notes

Book One, Part Two

Step Forward

Introduction to Part Two

Before you begin this next part, I invite you to reflect back to "day one" of your journey with the voice. It may seem like a long time ago...

There, you were met with tenderness, compassion, and love—qualities that have infused all of the lessons from that first day to this point. You received an invitation and were reminded to focus your mind. All along you have been comforted, encouraged, and reminded that you are worthy of love, and you matter so very much.

Being human, we will circle back to having days when we need reminders. We won't always feel "full" and sunny inside, and our mind will sometimes venture off in its own direction. We must not berate ourselves when these things happen. We have tools to manage our way through, and Part One remains at our fingertips for those times when the hurt inside returns, the runaway mind takes over, or we just need to be reminded, again, of our value and worth.

In Part Two, the voice meets us a little further down the path toward healing and becoming. We are up and out of the mud, and ready to receive actionable lessons. From here we will step further into becoming who we really are, and who we are meant to be.

I am especially excited to introduce you to the Morning Exercise in this section, Lesson 33. It is a wonderful way to start each day in order to *set the day*. But first, another lesson on what is Real ...

9

Cleanse, Fill, and Receive

Lesson 32: Draw in the Power of Real

And so it is ...

On this day, know and remember that you are a living, breathing, and moving aspect of spirit itself, contained in a human body—your vessel.

When you stand, draw Real power and strength up through the bottoms of your feet, up and out from the raw, pure energy that emanates from the core of the earth.

Walk in the knowing that each time your foot connects with and touches the earth, a part of this pure energy is transferred into your being. *This is the Power of God.*

Feel the air around you, the touch of the breeze as it gently caresses your skin and softens the moment. *In this is the Hand of God.*

See the sun and know its heat as it travels through you and warms your being. As it fills you, know that *this is the Essence of God.*

Listen to the birds, the trees swaying, the quiet, for *this is the Music of God.*

"And So It Is"

This is really all that is Real.

The commotion, the stress, and the details of daily living ... they are but distractions.

In the material world they have purpose, but you are ready for and desirous of moving beyond that which is readily seen. You are ready to find truth.

In solitude, in quiet, in peace, in that knowing place within, you find what is Real.

The more you come here for filling, the more you can receive.

The more you come here for filling, the quieter the noise in your world and the more limited your rushing.

Lesson 33: Morning Exercise

And so it is ...
Good morning. It is a beautiful day! Let's begin.

Begin
As you walk, allow yourself to quiet within and become aware.

Center your thoughts and calm the mind. Look around you: see, sense, be, breathe in and breathe out. Think about all that is good in your life and all that you have to be grateful for. Breathe in and breathe out, and walk on. Express your gratitude: For this day, this moment, this time to connect to what is Real. For your capacity to set your day and create a day of your own choosing. For these things and whatever else you are grateful for. Thank the Universe, your Higher Power as you define it, or whomever you speak to on *your* walk. Name all the things you are grateful for as they come to mind.

Focus now on your feet—on standing purposefully and consciously in your feet. They connect you to the earth. They support your vessel—they are the foundation of you.

Observe yourself from above as you stand in your feet and step forward. See yourself grounded and strong. See yourself stepping forward.

"And So It Is"

As you walk, notice each step you take, observing yourself walking on and stepping forward. Sense yourself standing in your feet, present in them.

From this place of conscious attention to being grounded in your feet, draw down, from the bottoms of your feet—as if two electric cords are extended from them—to the core of the earth. Draw down to this bubbling core, the perpetual motion and power within the center of the earth. This motion and power never cease, and you are part of the power.

Connect yourself to this energy—plug into it—and *pull* the power, might, light, and strength up and into your being. Into your feet, your calves, your thighs, your torso, down your arms, into your fingers, up into your head. Pull this energy up throughout all of you. Feel it as it courses through your vessel.

See this energy as it whooshes through you, cleanses you, and washes away all that is harmful to your well-being. Let it wash away anything that bothers your mind from yesterday, anything that weighs you down. Let this power from the earth cleanse anything that has become attached to your vessel—"stuff" you carry around: fear, chatter, regret, shame, resentments, old stories of who and what you are, what someone else said or did, analysis of current and perhaps difficult situations you find yourself in today. See it washed away.

See this energy as it covers all the shadow within you, and chases it away. Let all the shadow be washed away by this powerful light and energy from deep within the planet's core. Feel this energy as it cleanses your vessel of any distractions you carry. Use this energy from the perpetual power of the core of the earth to scrub your mind and your vessel. Cleanse yourself within, that you might begin your day fresh and new.

Know that your vessel—that which you call "body"—is cleansed through this exercise. And all darkness and shadow are washed away by the light coursing through you; you are free.

Stand in your feet and visualize this cleansing and releasing.

Stand in this peace, knowing that your vessel is void of all darkness, shadow, and negativity.

Breathe in and breathe out.

It is time to fill.

Move in your mind to the top of your head. Open the channel on the top of your head, that your vessel can be filled with light. Feel light being poured into you. See yourself being filled from above. You are filled first in your toes, then your feet, ankles, calves, thighs, until your whole body is filled with light up to the top of your head.

Stand in the knowledge that you are void of darkness, and full of light.

Feel the grounding of your being as you stand solid in your feet, having received light from above. Feel how full, complete, whole, and strong you are. See that there is room for nothing but this light in your vessel.

Plug any energetic holes in your vessel with your thoughts, so your vessel can hold this light and it does not seep out from you.

Breathe in; breathe out. Stand in this. Be one with this.

You are cleansed.

You are filled.

Here ends Step 1 of the Morning Exercise.

"And So It Is"

Continue

From this place of roundness, fullness, wholeness, and completeness, from here: Rise up. Straighten your spine, lift your chin and your eyes, pull your shoulders back, and literally raise your sight line—see what is in front of you, but see it as if your eyes are above your head. See from *here*—not from the eyes you are accustomed to using. Rise up—see from *here*, from this higher place, from your essence, and from your being.

See the beauty of all surrounding you.

Seek to see and know that which is Real and true—it is all around you.

Feel the warmth.

Breathe in more light; breathe out all else.

Hear the beautiful angelic voices; they are all within you.

Remember who you really are.

Remember *what* you really are.

Know—in this moment and in all moments—you are one with All.

You are a spirit.

You are spirit in a human body.

Rise up again. See more. See what is around you, but seek to see more: see beyond what obviously presents. That which you see is but physical manifestation of energy. See more. See the energy of the things around you. See truth, beauty, light. Feel Real strength and Real power as they come to you from deep within the core of the earth.

Now, look in front of you: Meet your Higher Self, who is standing in front of you to join with you on your journey today. She welcomes you, he awaits you. They stand regal in royal dress replete with cloak and crown. Greet them. If you do not know their name, ask them. Ask them how to reconnect with them this morning. To be joined, and walk through your day as one, how are you to become one? Are you to step into them? Will they step into you? Not all days will be the same … In whatever way you will merge today with your Higher Self, allow the merging to happen.

If you are to step into them, do so now.

And, if they are to step into you, do so also, and then allow them to place your crown and cloak upon you.

Notice how tall and straight you stand. Notice how strong and filled with Real power you are.

Aa-aa-aah. You have met and reunited with your Higher Self.

You have merged your wounded self with who you are intended to be. This is who you are.

Rise up. Stand as your royal, highest self.

Then: Step forward, approaching your day from the place of strength, highest purpose, highest thoughts, best you. Bring this thought energy of who and what and how you are into each part of this day.

Here ends Step 2 of the exercise.

Go Deeper
Step forward, one foot in front of the other, connected to the earth, in your feet, aware of being one with your Higher Self. Observe yourself from above, seeing yourself walk on.

As you step forward, know your path is blessed. The ground under your feet and ahead of you is sacred, bathed in light and radiating light and love and Real power.

As you step forward, take my hand—I am here.

As you step forward, take God's hand—s/he is here.

Step forward—holding hands with both of us—knowing that as you walk, reunited with your Higher Self, you are also connected with God and me, your teacher. We are light, and as you hold our hands, we can transfer more light into your vessel, that you remain filled, that you remain connected. At any time throughout the day, squeeze our hands and you will receive more light. You are surrounded by illumined radiance. You are connected to the All.

Remember who you really are.
Step forward into your day from this place.
Tall.
Strong.
Shoulders back, chin up, eyes up, grounded in your feet.
Cleansed.
Filled with light.
One with All.
Knowing who you really are.

Not caught up in daily distractions, but able to transcend and bring that which is Real to all situations, all people, all places. Able to be in this place of roundness, fullness, wholeness, and completeness. Filled. Standing in your feet.

You and I are one. We are all one.
Walk in light.
Walk tall.
Remember who you are.

Stand in this Real power. Stand strong. Stand in your feet. Aware of your connection to the earth. Dismiss any runaway thoughts that flit through your head. Get back into your feet. Stand strong, connected, one with All, firmly planted, secure. As your day unfolds and chatter enters your mind, remind yourself to remain grounded and secure. Tell yourself:

If I am in my head, I cannot be in my feet.
Be in your feet today. Be not in your head.
Remember who you are.

Rise up.
Step forward.
Fall back not.

"And So It Is"

Lesson 34: Allow Your Gifts to Unfold

In the Morning Exercise, we are taught to cleanse and fill our vessel—*set our day*—so that we might live from our Highest Self. The voice instructs us to do this every day. Over time, like a rock in a rushing river, our shape is changed—and we slowly release all that holds us back from being able to receive and live our grandest life.

Today's lesson speaks of shedding the shadows and *removing the curtain we have kept drawn as a protective barrier between ourselves and happiness*. Drawing back the curtain is a further step in cleansing ourselves. The curtain—the separating veil—that cloaks the clarity of a new life is easy to remove. Simply see it (or if you cannot see it, become aware of its presence). *And then open it.* That's it; just open it. If you'd like, add this as a step in your own Morning Exercise. It is most important to rid ourselves of anything and everything we carry within that separates us from being able to live a life of our own choosing each day. It *frees* us.

The voice tells us that when we strip away the things inside us that maintain barriers, we are able to step into the beginning of a new future. The curtain may have been drawn when we lived in fear, or were coping with trauma. *With this new image, the voice invites us to let go of the ways we have shrouded and protected ourselves so that nothing and no one could get inside and harm us again.* That we no longer need this curtain of separation and protection is such welcome news.

As we cleanse and remove barriers, we are able to grow beyond yesterday and the scar tissue of the past. We connect to that deep, knowing place inside us where we experience quiet calm. We shift inside, and sink into truth. Over time, anything not of this ceases to matter.

Today, *throw open the curtain* and naturally discover and step further into who you really are. Filled, whole, complete and one with truth and beauty, light, oneness, and real love.

And so it is ...

Good morning, dear one. How lovely is this day. You are brighter, lighter, and sunnier inside.

You are shedding the shadows that have lingered inside and around your being. Shadows that had cast darkness where there ought to be light, fear where there ought to be strength and confidence, and insecurity and doubt when you thought to take a new step.

Fear not.

For so long, you have kept a curtain drawn as a protective barrier between yourself and happiness.

Remove the curtain. Allow the open-air freedom of moving beyond protection and fear to become your new way of being.

As you strip away the things inside you that maintain barriers, you are able to step into the beginning of a new future. A future where you are brimming with real confidence, real strength, real truth, real love, and the ability to bring real connection to those you meet.

You have nothing to fear.

"And So It Is"

Your healing is accelerating.

Your change is quickening.

Your cells are vibrating more rapidly.

The energy you bring to your day is more productive and powerful.

Fear not.

Analyze this not.

Allow the unfolding of your gifts to proceed as a beautiful flower blossom unfolds.

Connect to that deep, knowing place inside where nothing but truth resides. That knowing place where only pure energy exists, and you are one with All and with the energy of Real love.

As you stand in this sacred space and sacred time, breathe it in, smell it, hear the angelic sound of it, and be filled entirely with it.

As you are renewed, allow nothing else to come near you. No thought of lack, no questioning of purpose, no worry of what will be.

Stand in this place and be filled.

The quieting that overcomes you and surrounds you is truth, beauty, and pure love.

By placing yourself in this sacred, knowing space, you return to your original, ethereal, Real home. From the nurturing here, you can step back into your human home a more complete person.

You are separate from the Universe right now—you are in human form. But this recharging feeds you as no other and nothing else can.

From this place of reenergizing, your eyes are changed, your mind is renewed, your heart is filled, and you cannot embrace any feeling of lack or unworthiness in any way.

For here you are reminded that any feeling or thought

of lack is not Real. Lack is not possible, not when you know you are part of the I Am, the Infinite.

And you shall walk on this earth as more than mere human, remembering who and what you really are.

Notes

10

Go Forth

Lesson 35: Recognize Separation

Today we continue to practice living in a state of conscious awareness, focusing the mind on what matters. We seek wholeness, fullness, and completion within—ready to face the day, regardless of what it entails.

As we become more aware of our connection to the All and allow ourselves to realize that connection more frequently, the colors within our hearts and the spectrum of our lives naturally widen and broaden.

Of course, it is difficult, if not impossible, to live in this state of acute awareness at all times. Today the voice teaches that if we can but feel it when we stray from this state of awareness, we have the power to come back.

He gives us the perfect diagnosis to know when the straying has happened: if we feel lack or self-doubt or unworthiness, or if we lose the feeling of wholeness, fullness, and completeness within, the straying has happened.

"And So It Is"

Today, we challenge ourselves to be aware of the moments—and our presence within them.

When we realize our minds have strayed from the moment at hand, we are invited to be grateful for noticing, to not berate ourselves, and to simply reconnect.

And so it is ...
You and I are one.
We are all one.
There is no separation. There is not a place where you begin and end that is not of me. We are one.

In this knowing, in this state of being, when living from this place, this space of roundness and fullness and "all things are possible," you have no room for separation and lack. You know and experience Real acceptance and create love in every place you are and with all you encounter.

Feel it when you stray from this place.

You will know you have strayed if you are alert to the moment. Anything other than this feeling of completeness means separation and division, and that you have stepped away and are back into the familiar, where the messaging is of lack and mistrust and fear.

See it immediately. Judge yourself not. Just tell it, *Not today—not now—please go from here. There exists no room for you today.* Then ...

Be grateful:

Grateful for being able to recognize you have fallen back into the past.

Grateful for being able to send darkness and limitation away from you.

Grateful for not falling prey to doubt and fear.

Grateful that love is here, and that you are gradually becoming more comfortable residing in what is Real and true and less and less comfortable with pain and shadow.

It is right. The time is here. Allow this opening to the new to occur. See the colors of your heart and the spectrum of your life broaden. There is naught but light ahead if you will but receive.

"And So It Is"

Lesson 36: Do Not Reach Back

The life-changing wisdom imbedded within these lessons naturally expands over time. When we shed the false self and the attachments that blind us, our eyes become able to see what is Real and we become who we really are. We are then able to comprehend these truths on a much deeper level.

Retraining the mind takes time.

Learning to *live these truths* takes practice.

We do not seek perfection, but progress.

"Becoming" happens.

Today, let this lesson become one with you.

Let yourself feel the words as you read them.

Let yourself become so magnificently filled that today, nothing but this love consumes you.

And so it is …

You come to this day as spirit, remembering who you really are.

You live on earth, but you are so connected to the I Am that all but that which is Real, true, and beautiful falls away, and you are one with your purest form.

You are filled so magnificently that there is no room for darkness, shadow, doubt, fear, self-doubt, or worry.

Go Forth

All that is Real is found in this place.
Remember the other not.
Do not reach back to the fear, darkness, and doubt.
Stand in this place of love and be filled and go forth.

Lesson 37: Stop the Stopping

And so it is ...

Release yourself fully into the passions I put into your mind. Do not say, "No." Do not say, "I cannot."

Do not limit yourself by overthinking. Allow me to be within your mind fully so the colors I envision for you, the pictures I paint, are created and manifested in your reality. You stop the process when you say, "I cannot," when you question how, when you act as if you can't see it happening. Stop the stopping. Allow the colors of my vision to spread and grow and become the picturesque reality of beauty, comfort, joy, and vitality. It is Real. It is happening.

But as you release and allow me to blur into your consciousness, you may brake too quickly, before the image fully appears so you can see it. Trust me. Trust yourself. Trust that my vision is perfectly aligned with my vision of greatness for you.

Do not say no.

Limit me not. In doing so, you limit yourself.

Remove the damper. Lift the lid. Feel the opening of your eyes to truly see around the corner and beyond the turn. You keep shutting down before it begins. Let it be uncomfortable. Step into the new. Get off the path you have defined as "I must comprehend fully if I am to move." In order to see, you must realign to not comprehending. When you glimpse the step around the corner, you become afraid and you run back to safety. But there is naught to fear.

Rather than retreat to your familiar, closed room, breathe into what I show you. Your future is not more of the same. You must let go. You must breathe and exhale into the next step and then take it, and trust the way your foot lands. So long as your eyes remain fixed on me—feet moving forward—all will be well. Feel the anxiousness. Keep going anyway. You will be fine. You know how to go forward.

Rise up. Step forward. Fall back not.

To change our life, we change our mind. To change our mind, we ponder something new. The voice leads off with the words "Release yourself fully into the passions I put into your mind." (We are being given ideas.)

He tells us not to say *no* or *I cannot* when new ideas present themselves, and not to limit ourselves by overthinking. Allow it to be uncomfortable, he tells us, and *keep going anyway.*

We do not need to understand the destination fully before we move forward. We must take a new step—breathe into it, exhale into it, take the damn step, and trust that our foot will land.

Our future is not more of the same.

It is notable that while the voice teaches us to step forward through today's fears, we are simultaneously healing yesterday's …

"And So It Is"

Lesson 38: Rise Up

And so it is …
    Be still.

    Visit not the playground of the past that exists today only in your mind. Visit it not.

    Step away from using that past as a definition of who you are today.

    You are renewed.

    You are not the messages you have absorbed over the years.

    You are worthy.

    Your life is blessed. Look upon me and allow me to send you light and love.

    Rise up.

This lesson reminds me of a story a friend shared with me years ago. He spoke of his past as being like a bad neighborhood—one that should not be visited, and one that is not safe for anyone to visit. He said that he used to go there all the time in his mind, and when he came back out, he again wondered why he had gone there *once again*. He has a tremendous sense of humor, and his delivery of the story was quite funny. I cannot convey his humor, but the message remains the same. All of us have places from our past that we visit in our minds—the voice calls it a *playground*; my friend called it a *bad neighborhood*. Whatever we call it, we are better off if we do not go visit it in our mind anymore. I am more susceptible to my mind wandering to the past—that old playground—when I am tired or when I am paying too much attention to situations around me. It wasn't very much fun to play there all those years ago; it certainly isn't any more fun today.

The voice reminds us that staying out of yesterday's playground—and staying present in the moment at hand—is a most worthwhile ambition. If you find yourself getting near the old neighborhood today, all you need to do is turn around. Today remains here for you. In all her splendor.

Lesson 39: You Are Forging a New Path

And so it is ...

Fall back not.

Not now. Not today.

Live in this moment. Do not conjure the shadows or pains of yesterday.

Walk tall, proud, and strong into this new way of being and living, stepping forward in this new direction.

Fear not.

Capture what I tell you.

Get these thoughts.

It is not a race, but you will not get around the corner in retreat.

You must allow the discomfort to lead you rather than dissuade you.

I am here. You are not foolish and will not step into harm, but you are more cautious than serves you today.

Step forward.

I have your hand. You do not need to have all the answers. I will show you the steps as you are ready for them. Listen. Breathe. Step forward. Push through the discomfort, and as you repeatedly forge ahead, a new path will be laid and you will find yourself gazing upon a new vista.

The journey is now. You are on the right track. Fear not, for I am with you.

Rise up. Step forward. Fall back not.
Today you can touch the temple of heaven. Trust me.

On this journey, we are asked to step forward and away from the shadows that have marred our vision and held us back. We are told that the future is not more of the same. We are encouraged to keep going, even when the way is uncertain. We are reminded that even though we cannot see around the turn, it is there that our future lies, for tomorrow exists in a place we cannot see, know, or comprehend.

We are invited to live grounded, connected, and present in the moments of each day, as best we are able. We learn to step confidently and deliberately as the grandest version of ourselves that we can envision in each moment. And over time, if we dare to embrace this new way of being, our view will be new. It is not a race, but the voice is right: we will not get around the corner if we retreat.

Keep going. Listen. Breathe. Step forward. And step forward again. For it is around the turn that your future lies.

Notes

11

Live These Lessons

Lesson 40: Stand Tall

And so it is …

When your mind goes running, you lose your footing. You lose your balance. You lose your "self."

No one, no "thing," no circumstance, no event is worth your getting up into your head and forgetting who you are.

Let not the opinions of others mar your opinion of self.

Let not your need for approval limit your ability to function and be.

Seek not validation from others.

Seek approval from me and from within.

For seeking outside of self will keep you from finding yourself and your purpose.

Do not let your fears take over.

Stand tall, in your feet. Fill with light and face your day. Cower not.

Do not think of others more highly. For you are the only one who can bring your perspective and your gifts.

"And So It Is"

> Do not aim to be like another. Your job—being you—is big enough.
>
> Let validation come only from me and your Higher Self.
>
> We will not lie to you or judge you.

❖

Some common themes in this lesson:

Stop the running mind. When it takes off, you lose your footing.

Stand in your feet.

No person, place, or thing is worth getting all up into your head about and forgetting who you are.

The opinions that (you think) other people hold of you ought not mar the opinion you hold of yourself. Ever.

Do not let your *need for approval* sway what you think or do, or hinder your ability to get through the day.

Do not even *seek* approval from others. If you believe you are doing the next right thing, chances are, you are.

Do not allow fear to take over—*get in your feet*. Stand tall, fill with light, and face the day!

Do not cower! Stand straight, shoulders back, chin up, eyes up, exuding confidence from within.

Do not think anyone else is better than you.

Be you.

Seek validation from your Higher Self, not others.

Smile …

You are doing just fine.

Lesson 41: Leave Sunshine in Your Wake

And so it is ...

Fear not. Do not lead your day with anything but these truths.

Frustrate not. Tolerate more. Listen more.

You will see those who are like you and those who are not.

You will see those who remember who they really are. Seek them.

Do not allow those who are unlike you to frustrate you. See them. Understand. Bring light and love. And gently walk on. Leave only sunshine of spirit, not darkness or shadow, in your wake.

In the simplicity of this lesson, we are reminded of so much.

It is not surprising that the voice leads off with *Fear not. Begin your day with these truths.* I think this means *all* of his truths: to stand in our feet, cleanse and fill, focus on what we can control; to rise up and operate from our Higher Self, not our wounded self, and to step forward and not fall back into old habits, to name just a few.

Here, in this lesson, he adds to his quiver of truths: We are to *frustrate not, tolerate more, and listen more*. When we are connected to our Source, have set our day, and operate from a place of wholeness and fullness within, it is natural to be able to do these things.

"And So It Is"

We are each on our own path and our own timetable of healing and awakening, walking our own unique journey. This lesson encourages us to seek those who are like us, accept those who are not, frustrate not (*set the mind*), see people as they are, understand, and leave behind only light and love.

The voice inspires us and invites us to walk away from all encounters gently—not in a huff—leaving only sunshine in our wake.

Hmmm.

It is easier to do this on some days than it is on other days—and it is very good to remember that we seek progress, not perfection.

Let's notice and celebrate ourselves on the days when we do this well. Let's try to have gratitude on the days when we remember to try but do it perhaps clumsily or awkwardly.

And on the days when we forget the lesson entirely, let's readily forgive our humanness, make amends as needed, and fortify ourselves to try to do better next time.

Lesson 42: See That Which Matters

And so it is ...

Daily turmoil and stressors are but small details within what really matters. But until you know to look for what really matters, you will see only the insignificant, the petty, the irritating, the small things of this earth. Awaken, and discern the difference between Real and unreal, truth and untruth, important ("really matters" important) and that which takes your eyes off the ball—that which seems important but is only a distraction.

Get out of the mode of cause and effect.

Step away from the distractions and focus on all things true and Real. Rise up. Lift your eyes higher and keep them open by seeing from your essence, your being, by seeing that which is Real.

When you see your day, walk your path, and look upon others from this vantage, all else falls away and that which is not Real also falls away.

From this place, you are in Spirit. You are in strength. You see more here than what can be readily seen; you see the essence of what is Real. You are one with All.

Let the things that are not Real go—things that are of earthly binding only and not of truth. Let them all go.

Sit with me.

When you speak, be aware of what you utter. Let the useless words fade away. Spend more time wondering what

I would have you say and do in the moment, and less time making casual chitchat.

Bring me with you wherever you go.

Speak from the place where you know you are one with me, and one with All Consciousness. Speak from here.

Be one with me in all times and all situations and you will find your true self, your essence, your healing—for there is nothing but pure energy here.

Here, things in the past fall away.

Pain from the past, fear of the future, shame, fear, doubt, arrogance, division, insecurity about self—all these things fall away because they do not exist in the I Am. They cannot be present because they are only earthly, and they only exist due to lack.

Lack does not exist in the I Am.

It is outside the whole.

Does it exist? Yes!

But it is not found in the I Am.

And so the question is how to change your life. The answer, "Change your mind," is true and Real!

Rise up. Step forward. Fall back not.

This means something! This is instructional!

Rise up out of the illusion of separation and lack.

Step forward in faith into and with the I Am, into the whole of All—and stay there if you can. This is the "fall back not."

Fall back not into limitation.

Fall back not into forgetting you are one with All, and on this earth but not of it.

This one is a tall order, but inspiring.

    Ground yourself into what is Real, that all else falls away.

    Rise up out of the illusion of separation and lack. Step forward.

    The voice will speak at length to this concept in Book Two.

    For today, practice staying in your feet, and connect to what is Real before you speak.

    Awake.

    Aware.

    Conscious.

    Connected more to this practice than to the chatter in your head and the situations surrounding you. Focused first, connected second, speaking third.

"And So It Is"

Lesson 43: Let Troubles Fall Away

And so it is ...
Lean into me.
Worry not.
Let all that troubles you fall away.
Fill yourself, instead, with light. Let all shadow within, all hurt, and all sadness fall away. And inside, you smile again and shine again.
Let the behaviors of others harm you not.
Their own fears and pain and unresolved yesterdays sometimes erupt.
Do not take them on.
Do not take their pain.

Learning to stand tall, strong, connected, whole, and full is a strategy enabling us to be less regulated by other people's behavior—so our mood and responses and the quality of our day are not governed by another person.

It is easy to react.

In this lesson the voice says: *Let the behaviors of others harm you not* and *Their own fears and pain and unresolved yesterdays sometimes erupt.*

I have read this truth many, many times, from many different sources; likely, we all have. It is easy to understand it and agree with it. We know intellectually that we are not responsible for another person's behavior, and that we should not let another person's behavior govern our own. Yet when operating from a place of insecurity while also seeking approval, it is both easy and common to do just that.

To truly comprehend that we are not responsible for another's behavior is amazingly freeing.

To be able to be able to choose our own behavior is—well, life changing.

When we have filled with light and are connected to the All, if someone we love or someone we encounter by chance erupts on us, we do not need to take it personally, retaliate, or storm off. We have a choice. We get to choose our own behavior, regardless of the behavior of others. *We need not accept the trigger.*

We get to let go—leaving light and love in our wake, ruminating not.

And oddly enough … the more we are able to do this, the more those around us are also able to naturally heal their own pain within.

"And So It Is"

Lesson 44: Rise Up from Fatigue

And so it is ...
>As you fear, you fatigue.
>As you doubt yourself, you fatigue.
>As you worry, you fatigue.
>Rise up.
>Look out farther.
>Change perspective.
>Rise up.

Fatigue was not something the voice had spoken about before. I welcomed this lesson when it arrived because I have wondered about fatigue for years. Perhaps we all have. There have been times when I felt worn out but did not think I'd done anything to warrant the feeling of deep tiredness.

Today the voice helps us understand fatigue from an emotional point of view. He tells us that it happens when we allow our mind to wander into fear, doubt, or worry. Fatigue also happens, I believe, when we ruminate, or dance with resentments. Any and all of these thought patterns can cause our energy to drop into a lower frequency, leaving behind weariness, fatigue, and/or too much sensitivity—much like an emotional hangover. Once we have arrived in this lower wavelength, it takes work to cleanse (again), fill (again), and get back to where we were before we tangled with darkness.

This lesson offers a solution: to rise up and away from the thoughts that cause fatigue.

We are in charge of our soul's energy, and our frequency. To lift these up, we are to lift up our thoughts. Today we are inspired (again) to notice what we think about, and keep our mind focused so we can maintain the balance we seek.

"And So It Is"

Lesson 45: Your Answer Is Light

And so it is ...
    This day, this very day, all of life resides here.
    Cease diving back into yesterday.
    Stay away from obsessing about tomorrow.
        Be here
        in this moment
        in this day.
    Looking for and seeing light, truth, and beauty.
    Let all else fall away.
    When in doubt, bring light.
    When in fear, claim light.
    When in sadness, bathe in light.
    When in anger, rest in light.
    Your answer is light.
    All else is unreal.

I'm sure someone must have said, "*This day, this very day, all of life resides here*" before I scribed the same sentence for the voice. This would make sense since it is such an important concept. Many things the voice tells us are intended to remind us of something we already know. It's been said that to change a paradigm, a person needs to hear a new thought over and over and over again before they even realize the new thought has been presented. This is what we are doing here: shifting paradigms. It is common to repeat the same thoughts so often that we no longer hear them—but we are governed by them. If we wish to awaken to a new way of living, it is time for new thoughts.

Today the voice challenges us to wake up to light, truth, and beauty. To wake up and recall the melody of a long-forgotten song and lend our voices to the chorus of pure light. To wake up and embrace who and what we really are, and reside as one—connected to the divine.

All else is unreal.

Notes

12

Deepen Your Practice

Lesson 46: Set Running Thoughts Aside

And so it is ...

Worry not. Do not think too hard on the thoughts bubbling inside. Leave them; set them aside. Allow nothing but that which is pure, true, and fulfilling to occupy you.

All else is nonsense. All else is but distraction from creating the day of your choosing. All else creates separation and angst.

All that is pure and true is blasted away by the noise of that which is unreal.

Look away. Tell your mind to stop running, and get grounded again into what is Real.

As you do, you will straighten in your walk. You will align your spine and function with more strength and power.

Flitting thoughts drive an empty life, eyes unable to focus, anxiety in body.

Set running thoughts aside. Do not allow them to occupy you, as they will take over and destroy your day.

"And So It Is"

Send them on their way and rest, and be in my peace and strength.

The mind is a powerful thing. Many of us have needed much work and practice to become aware of it and manage it.

Ruminating, worrying, bubbling thoughts are not productive, and as the voice describes so well here, they are a distraction: *nonsensical and noisy*. The noise of the mind will blast away all that is pure and true.

How ought we manage our way through?

The voice tells us again: *Look away*. Stop the runaway mind. Stand tall and straight, grounded in our feet, standing present in life-giving thoughts.

Lesson 47: Remember Who You Really Are

And so it is ...
>Wake up.
>Reach deeply.
>Sink into me, into quiet, into peace.
>Stay away from mindless chatter in your head.
>Ground yourself fully onto the earth by focusing on being present and sturdy in your feet.
>Breathe from this place.
>Stand in this place.
>Know that all may swirl around you but you are grounded in my protection, Real strength, and power.
>Do not leave this place.
>When you are faced with tense situations, difficult people and relationships, and obsessive thoughts, when you center on and swirl around "what-ifs" in your head, stop your mind and come back to your feet.
>Berate yourself not—for you will never be perfect, nor will anyone else journeying this path of self-knowledge and becoming.
>It is an ebb and flow, this learning.
>Never perfect but never meant for perfection.
>Growing daily.
>Changing always.
>More accepting of self each day.

"And So It Is"

> Remember who you Really are, my dear.
> Be gentle with yourself in your becoming.

Interesting first sentence in today's lesson: *Wake up*.

For a long time I thought it meant "wake up in the morning" to this fresh, new day. To sit up, stretch, get out of bed, put on a pot of coffee or tea, and begin the day.

Funny how these lessons go.

Now I don't think he meant anything like what I first imagined.

We have embarked on what may be our most important journey in life. We are releasing, awakening, and becoming. *One might say we are waking up.* It is our time, and it's here and it's now.

Over time, these lessons will also wake up for us in a new way. Sometimes it might feel as if they have been rewritten, and we wonder, "When did *that* message get in here?" And of course, the text hasn't changed at all but we have become capable of deeper comprehension. The layers and depth of meaning are there, and they are embedded throughout all of the lessons in this book. In time they will reveal themselves—not because they change, *but because we change*. The voice tells us in Book Two: *As you see so shall you be*. When we strip away what blinds us, we become able to see and know.

We ground—to connect to and release into what is Real.

We sink into calm—to quiet the mind and to hear.

We step forward on our journey—not perfectly, but as we are able—being gentle with ourselves at all times as we go.

The first three sentences of this lesson are a powerful invitation to furthering our awakening. Challenge yourself to live in this way today:

Awake.

Reaching deeply.

Sinking into quiet, sinking into peace.

"And So It Is"

Lesson 48: Strengthen and Receive

And so it is ...
As you continue, you strengthen your vessel.
As your vessel strengthens, you can receive more light, abundance, strength, power, truth, beauty, and dignity.
You will not crack.
You hold these gifts. You shine more and you give more.
Let my light fill you.
Let my light cover the shadows within, that they will disappear.
Let my light give you peace—that as you live your moments of each day, you trust my lessons more and live from more peace and Real power.

The majority of these lessons focus on mind, psyche, and soul, but today we are reminded of another critical aspect of being—our vessel.

The voice tells us that as we continue with these lessons, we strengthen our vessel—a natural and necessary part of our practice. Our ability to grow is directly related to our ability to receive and our capacity to hold the gifts of spirit we have received. Often, the voice speaks about wholeness, completeness, and fullness within. It feels good to be in this place, but maintaining this sense of being requires focus, awareness, and strength.

The voice has recently expanded upon how to accomplish this. He likens our ability to "hold ourselves open" to the image of "puffing our vessel out" so our vessel remains strong, full, and as "round" as it is able to, the way our body expands after we slowly fill ourselves with air. Our shoulders naturally slide back into place, our posture aligns, our back and lungs broaden, and our breath is slow and deep, emanating from our diaphragm. As we breathe in and breathe out, and as we step through our day—at any time—we can focus on maintaining a "filled" vessel, as if we are "puffed out." In doing this, we stretch and strengthen our vessel, become able to retain more, and stand taller, broader, and more deliberately connected to our feet. This exercise develops and increases our capacity to hold our growing, flourishing, and expanding soul and self.

These are some of the things I think of when I read *you will not crack*. As our vessel fills with more light, abundance, strength, power, truth, beauty, and dignity, we must increase our vessel's capacity because *we can only carry as much as we are able to hold*.

Today, if you are not already, become aware of the soul-to-vessel connection. Commit to strengthening, bolstering, and streamlining your vessel each day.

"And So It Is"

Lesson 49: Embrace the Day

And so it is ...
  Today, a new day.
  Embrace it lovingly.
  Care for it.
  Caress it.
  Nurture it.
  All that is Real is here now, in this moment, in this new day.
  Be one with me as you walk through it.
  Eyes on me.
  Standing in your feet.
  Stepping forward.

Today's lesson is simple, direct, and easy to "get."

It is also an inspiring way to live.

For many of us, thinking of each day as something we are to embrace, care for, caress, and nurture might be a new and different concept. A new viewpoint. When we are living in emotional pain, depression, anxiety, fear, or trauma, it is not uncommon to *wish away the day*—wishing it would just pass and be over with. Hopefully, we are now in a place where even if shadowy thoughts and feelings are present, we can manage through, sink deeper into these truths, comprehend that "this too shall pass," and still care for and live with presence in the precious moments of this day we have been given.

One way to accomplish this is to make a habit of doing the first step of the Morning Exercise—naming the things you are grateful for—and repeating this practice throughout the day. If you are reading this, you have been given another day. It may not be a perfect one, and you may not yet be where you wish to be, but you are here with another chance to get it "more right" than you got it yesterday. If you can focus on the day as something to be embraced, cared for, and nurtured, chances are that while it might not unfold as you hoped, it will be a fine day nonetheless.

Early on, I shared that the voice told me I could not change my life if I did not change my mind. To change your life, he said, you must change how you think. This lesson is one small example of that. To change the quality of our day, we must change how we view it. For today, *choose this day*—all that is Real is found *here*—inside each moment within this day. Be inside each moment, *aware* of all that is good in your life, and *grateful* for everything. Embrace, care for, and nurture this day. It is all there is.

"And So It Is"

Lesson 50: Repeat the Mantras of Light

And so it is ...
Fear not.
Look upon situations less.
Cease worry.
Be the light.
See the light in all things.
Bring light.
Say to yourself, "Let there be light, let me be light, let me bring light."
And then go on.

Today we are reminded to focus the mind: to stop thinking on people, places, and things, to cease our worrying, and to instead focus on light. We are inspired to connect with light on an even deeper level by interacting with it through these three mantras:

"Let *there be* light,
Let *me be* light,
Let *me bring* light."

Once we are able to fully live each of these mantras, we are well on our way to transforming within. Living in this manner requires us to set down everything else—all things unreal and all distractions—and purposefully connect to our Highest Self, knowing that we are so much more than any circumstance around us or the noise in our head.

Let *there be* light: See it and source it.

Let *me be* light: Claim it and allow the *natural shift into a higher frequency* to occur.

Let *me bring* light: Purposefully radiate the light we carry within so brightly that we might touch another's soul.

This is a very good plan. Accomplishing it requires extreme focus and intentional living. It is unlikely that any of us will achieve this level of interplay with light constantly, but it is worthy of remembering and striving for throughout the day. Imagine the collective awakening that could be sparked across the globe if we each cultivated a purposeful connection to, and powerful application of, light.

"And So It Is"

Lesson 51: Clear the Dam

And so it is ...
    As you grow, the events of life become easier and lighter for you to carry.
    But when they are heavy, let them go.
    When your mind is burdensome, let go of your thoughts.
    When you are analyzing all, set that aside.
    The "flow" has been interrupted.
    Your mind and overthinking have dammed it up.
    Release the clenching.
    Stop the running mind.
    Get into your feet.
    And walk strongly—connected to the earth and to me.

We are human, and human we will remain while incarnated on earth.

There is never a straight trajectory toward "becoming." Despite diligent practice, things will again get heavy for us to carry, our mind will again become burdensome, and we will undoubtedly fall back into overanalyzing.

The voice reminds us (without berating) that when this happens, we have fallen into distractions, and we have ceased the flow of the All—it has become dammed up.

All we need do in these moments of clarity is to clear the dam:

Release the clenching, breathe, and stop the running mind. Get into our feet, fill with light ("puff out"), and ground ourselves again into what is Real.

Notes

13

All Is Well

Lesson 52: Let All Things Flow

And so it is ...
Do not think obsessively.
Judge not.
Have expectations only of yourself.
All else is madness.
You cannot control others.
Let the energy of all things flow around you and wash over you, and the current of all be uninterrupted by the labor of your thoughts.
Let go of need.
Let go of desire.
Let go of expectation.
Put yourself on the path.
Walk in your feet.
Eyes up.
Chin up.

"And So It Is"

>Shoulders back.
>Full of light.
>Lacking in nothing.

This lesson is another one that is easy to "get" and easy to agree with in concept. Many have written about expectations, recommending that we let go of them. It has been said that when we have expectations of other people, we have the possibility to become disappointed. Here, the voice tells us to have expectations only of ourselves.

"All else is madness."

"You cannot control others."

This lesson couples well with and serves as an extension to yesterday's lesson. We will not tame the mind perfectly, but it is helpful to remember that the mental activities mentioned above can provide for and create the perfect conditions for an emotional storm.

The voice gives us our solution: Let go; let the energy of all things flow around us and over us; and focus on grounding ourselves in these principles.

Lesson 53: Seek the Next Blossoming

I will leave these next two lessons to stand on their own ...

> *And so it is ...*
> Embrace this day.
> The new, the opportunity, another chance at living, yet again today.
> Embrace each moment and be in it fully.
> Seek light.
> Sink into the light, and from this place, step into your day.
> Understand that *this* is all that matters.
> Your yesterdays are gone; they are over.
> The shadows that linger: Release them. Release them all. Let them fall away from you, as dirt washes off your body in a shower.
> Let my light be that shower, that you will carry yesterday's pain, shame, regret, resentment, and fear no longer.
> It is time.
> As you hold so tightly and cling to these things—things that today are only in your mind—you become weighed down and you are unable to rise and fly.
> Let it go. Let it all go.
> As thoughts of dark memories emerge, gently ask them to leave you.

"And So It Is"

As feelings from difficult times arise, tell them they are no longer relevant for you in today's life and world.

As fear arises, be aware of it—but ask for clarity of sight and discernment of thought so you will not project old feelings and old memories onto today's experiences.

Ask for clear eyes.

Ask for eyes to see, to really see, and *ask to be able to filter using today's language, not the scar tissue of yesterday.*

From here can you soar.

From here can you blossom and find Real truth, beauty, and joy.

Your heart is ready.

Your life awaits.

No longer are you to be encumbered by yesterday.

Move on.

Let go of those whom you carry in your vessel with resentment. Send them on their way, that you may move forward into the garden of heavenly delight—this next blossoming place of your life.

It awaits.

It is Real.

It is yours—you need just step into the garden and all will be revealed, and the beauty, the growing blossoms, the fragrance of sweet perfume will surround you. And as you surround yourself in this truth and beauty, all will be revealed to you.

Joy.

Love.

Peace.

Laughter.

Wholeness, fullness, completeness.

All abundance.

It is your time.

Lesson 54: Settle into Peace

And so it is ...

This day, this now, this moment—it is yours.

And it is mine

For you are an earthly living embodiment of me and of the I Am.

Be open to me.

Be accepting of light.

Fill yourself with my light so that unrest, anxiety, fear, self-criticism, doubt, fear, fear, fear, fear—so they gently wash away from your being.

I bring peace.

I bring clarity.

I bring knowing.

I bring and am light.

Step into the sunshine of my spirit and allow me to fill you.

You doubt. Let it go.

Say instead, I am one with the I Am. I am one with All. No harm will or can come unto me.

I am filled.

I am protected.

I am nourished with the nectar of the Divine.

All is well.

Your mind runs to chatter; gently quiet it.

Lay it to rest, ask it to just be, shut the door on the

"And So It Is"

noise and distraction, and walk away. Tomorrow your mind can run amok. Not today.

Today, settle yourself into peace.

Sit, lie down, stand, walk, run, exercise, read, love, make love. Do your life, but do it from this core place of light, love, and peace.

Let that knowing part of you reign supreme in your being today.

Anything else is old stuff.

Anything else is keeping you separate from what is true, pure beauty, and Real joy.

Light up within.

Sink into this peace.

Lesson 55: Go and Bring Light

And so it is …

You do not go alone.

You go ahead of your troubles.

You go, feet strong, stepping forward, eyes up, chin up, shoulders back.

You go and I am with you.

You go and my light surrounds you, fills you, inspires you, protects you—even from the shadows within. You go and you bring me. You go and you bring All.

You go and you bring light.

You go, and when you stay outside self-judgment and self-doubt and worry, you are one with those you see.

Do not let those worries into your day and your moments.

Lead with light.

Radiate because naught else is within.

You go.

Rise up.

Step forward.

Fall back not.

"And So It Is"

When we began, the voice repeated that we are never alone. Now, as we near the end of Book One, he does not just tell us that we are never alone, but that *we do not go alone*, and that we go ahead of our troubles. The statement "You go ahead of your troubles" connotes that we actually move past and beyond them—that we have left them behind us. All these days later, and all these lessons later, we go: feet strong, stepping forward, eyes up, chin up, shoulders back. How marvelous it is to not be pitiful anymore. How marvelous it is to be up and out of the mud, going ahead of our troubles. Congratulations to us—we have found growth. We have found our feet.

In this lesson he says, "*You go, and when you stay outside self-judgment and self-doubt and worry, you are one with those you see.*" Think about that sentence. When we are living with (and in) self-judgment, self-doubt, and worry, it is not possible to connect with another. We become so wrapped up and entangled in our own fears and insecurities that we miss out on the many possible moments of connecting with another person—and leaving some light behind.

We strive to keep our self filled, that we are whole and complete, bringing radiance and light. Perhaps another person is in need of our light. Perhaps we are in need of theirs.

Today, go, feet strong, stepping forward, eyes up, chin up, shoulders back, filled with light, and radiant.

Do not miss the gift of connection that is intended for you today.

Lesson 56: All Is Well

And so it is …
    The day's end.
    Rest.
    Let today wash away as you recoup and prepare to begin again tomorrow morning.
    All is well.
    Peace surrounds within and without.
    Let me be one with you as you dream, as you leave and go unto other places.
    Rest.
    All is well.

    And so it is …
    And all is well.

A Closing Message to Book One from the Voice

And so it is ...
    We close this particular chapter of your healing. The growing, the healing, and the becoming never end, though, my dear.
    You began by releasing the wounds that left behind their bruises on your soul.
    You began by seeing yourself as more than you have been told you are, and knowing that you are more than the details of your life and the narrative of your "story."
    You have gained confidence and personal power. You have learned to quiet the chatter in your mind, and stand strong in your feet, strengthen your vessel, and practice basic steps each day to finally step away from darkness, shadow, pain, rumination, resentments, self-doubt, sadness, and all things unreal in order to live whole, full, complete, in Real power, and filled with light. It is a "step-full" process you take: You cannot move from living in pain and lack to amazing light power in one step. You grow day by day, a bit at a time, over a series of days strewn together, re-forging the path your feet tread to "become," as a flower germinates from seed to blossom.

"And So It Is"

It is not always perfect, and was never meant to be. Be gentle with yourself in your becoming, especially when growing pains present themselves.

As you go through your day, project your light ahead of you, at all times, in all situations, and in every encounter you have; purposefully radiate your light before you. See, actually *see* the light within you emanating from your vessel. And as you step forward, see yourself stepping into this light so it becomes one with you again. Imagine spraying perfume on the path ahead and then stepping into its fragrance.

When you intentionally lead with light, you naturally become more than you believe yourself to be. You are reminded of who and what you really are: a divine spirit, part of the whole, one with your Creator, a spirit living on the earth but not of it. You further the reconciling of your earthly self with your Higher Self. You live alert and present in the moment.

Your purpose is to awaken: You must remember who and what you really are. That you are not the details of your existence thus far—that is but a distraction. That is what you became when the separation of your soul occurred. The separation is a natural process of the soul when incarnating into human form. As you progress, as you step away from illusion and step into your Higher Self and the ways of truth, beauty, and pure knowledge, you are given glimpses of the ethereal while living on earth.

Stay away from chatter.
Stay away from darkness.
Do not ponder the details of the past.
Ruminate not.
Focus.
Pay attention.
Rise up: Stand strong in your feet, straighten your spine,

lift your chin and your eyes, and see from here. Purposefully meet your Higher Self, and reconnect with your Real self and your life force. As you step forward and walk through your day, direct your thoughts to cast your light out in front of you; and as you do this repeatedly, you will meld further into your true being, and you will fall back into shadow less and less.

Do not forget these lessons. But if you do, I am here.
I am always here. Take my hand. I am always with you.
And so it is, and all is well.

Notes

Book Two

Find Your Way Home—
Transform Yourself
and the World

Introduction to Book Two: A Message from the Voice

And so it is …

On this day we move to a different level of learning.

In Book One we spent much time on self-worth: Learning to see yourself as worthy, loved, beautiful, radiant, strong, and one with All. That you are more than your past and your "story." That you are so much more than you have been told you are, and so much more than you have ever believed yourself to be.

There began your lessons. For if you are unable to believe you matter and are worthy, if you are unable to believe and know who and what you really are—a spirit incarnated in human flesh—you cannot accept the lessons contained in this volume.

There is a wide spectrum of souls living on your planet. You might call this spectrum a hierarchy of awakening, or a stepladder toward opening to what is Real.

Each one of you is on this continuum, on your own rung of awakening. Each progressing in your own perfect time, as intended. Many of you seek to rise and connect to what is Real. To live from your highest self, and to comprehend, at the deepest level within, what cannot be understood.

To those of you who seek, I say: come here, to this place. When you learn to live from *this* place, you will be able to see the path of light upon which you walk; transcend the daily, petty, sometimes nonsensical situations humans experience; and live fully grounded in what is Real while simultaneously rising up into who you really are. From here, you will naturally share your gifts, fulfill your purpose, and deliver your destiny.

When you learn to live from *this* place, ego is overcome.

When you learn to live from this place, fear, doubt, worry, and shadow are washed away. All that is not Real is washed away. You become reconciled with your Higher Self—your Real self—and you live in, and from, Real power.

Each day you must cleanse your vessel of shadows and distractions that have attached themselves to you like barnacles. When they remain attached to your vessel and your mind, it is difficult if not impossible to step forward into the concepts laid out in this book. Therefore, cleanse within each day, because attachment is elemental to being human.

You become attached; things attach to you.

The lower self seeks attachment, which provides security, safety, and identity, but nothing Real.

Attachment binds you to earthly concepts.

When you are out of attachment—living from the place where you see and seek from your essence, from the eyes of your soul—you are free to deepen and rise and find what is Real.

Cleanse within each day to tame ego. It is strong, and it wants control. It wants to reign supreme.

As you cleanse yourself of attachments and ego, you can lose the things that exist on the lower rungs of the ladder of awareness.

Remove self from mind,

Remove ego from vessel,

Remove shadow,
Remove distractions and attachments,
Add and focus upon what is Real.
These are the goals.

When you cleanse with light each morning, you release the habit of keeping the soul connected to the material and physical, and you can learn to align with what is Real.

This is the hierarchy: As your soul remains connected to earthly attachments and ego, you reside on a lower rung of awareness. Hierarchical gain is achieved by counterintuitive measures—earthly power and politics do not assist in the growth, awakening, and achievement of the royal status of the soul.

Removal of mind, ego, and attachment brings—
Real dignity,
Full abundance,
Radiant light,
Immense power,
True beauty,
Pure heart,
Connection of self to the whole,
And the reunification of soul with home.

Welcome. *In this second book you will find your home and fulfill the longing of the soul.* You will learn to be in your Real home even as you reside on earth. When you can comprehend, you complete the circle. When you gain the ability to grasp these concepts that are beyond comprehension, you will know how to remain home while residing on earth. Your "ah-hah!" will not be as a light flickering. It will become a deep calm into which you sink. You will release into it.

"And So It Is"

You will fall gently into Real truth. You will know that nothing in the world in which you reside is Real, but all is present nonetheless. That what you carry is what binds you. That what you believe to be true is only true in part. To grow, you must release from what you believe is true. To receive the new, you must understand why you have repelled receiving thus far. This is not a trick of the mind but a *fall* and a *release* into the Real knowledge that will come.

The beliefs, memories, imprints you carry are what bind you. They are the barnacles that attach, and carrying them upon your vessel means you cannot carry the new.

This is why if you are to grow, you must first wither.

To receive the new you must set down what you have been carrying, even what you have been unaware you are carrying.

It will arrive, this knowledge.

You will comprehend it within.

Rush not.

Force not.

Allow my truths to wash over you, through you, and carry you as if you are in a river of truth. And soon, very soon, you will see.

But to *see*, you must cease seeing as you see today.

To *know*, you must be willing to allow deeper comprehension to arrive.

As you see, so shall you be.

Let these truths wash over you.

Sit quietly with them.

Analyze them not.

They will fall into place for you as you allow the release.

Author's Introduction to Book Two

This first series of lessons in Book Two is foundational to the remainder of this volume of work. They are important because they establish the vernacular and imagery with which the voice underscores his remaining lessons.

In Book One, the voice inspired us to awaken.

Now, in Book Two, he leads us into the esoteric, into the powerful reality that lies behind, beneath, and within our material world. He submits that nothing we see readily with our human eyes is Real—that these things are visible, and they are present, but they are not Real, and that there is so much more for us to behold if we will but strip away what blinds us. He teaches us how to be able to see what is Real, and he describes what is Real using vivid imagery. He invites us to become able to comprehend and place ourselves in this place that is Real—a place he calls *home*—our soul's home.

In this collection of lessons, the voice uses different terms to describe *home*. He calls it *Real*, the *Temple of God*, and the *River (of Light)*. He introduces us to *light beings*, and leads us to understand that they are ethereal beings that have been with us for all time. We come to know that they have patiently awaited our awakening and our return home, so we can interact with them during the remainder of our walk on earth. You may envision and use the term *angels or guardians* instead of light beings—you may envision and use various other words to describe these ethereal concepts, as the voice could not possibly use the exact terms each person reading

"And So It Is"

this book most desires. So if the term light beings or another turn of phrase proves to be an obstacle, please feel free to substitute terms that are most meaningful to you. *The universal truths are not in the names but in the essence of the messages.*

Regardless of the words used, we are invited to see our physical world in a new way, and as more than what is readily apparent. By learning to see in this new way, the voice submits, we will be able to live an enhanced life. *"As you see, so shall you be"* and *"As you are, so is your life"* are two important phrases that he sprinkles throughout the remainder of the book. They clearly remind us to pay attention to our thoughts and our minds. If we see only lack, that is what we will create. But if we see and stand in truth, beauty, strength, real power, abundance, hope, joy, and all things lovely, we will create these states.

In this first section of Book Two, the voice repeats himself—a lot—and in fact, some passages may seem very long-winded. However, this section is tremendously important, and the repetition is purposeful. The voice is attempting an explanation of the ethereal (what he calls *Real*) for those of us who no longer remember.

With this word painting, he describes our physical realm in a new way, inviting us to see all that surrounds us differently, creating a foundational change in how we approach our perspective on this material realm and how we reside in it. Once we are able to see differently, he then leads us to mentally reside in this place of the ethereal within, garnering its power.

I considered shortening this section because of its repetition, but throughout the book I have diligently tried to leave his lessons as close as possible to how they were given. The concepts he provided and the directions he took did not always make sense to me as I was receiving them, yet I have later found he has picked up those strands of wisdom again and woven them to completion.

That is what is happening here in this first section. He puts it all out there, deliberately and sometimes painstakingly describing the concept of *home*, the *river*, the *temple within*, and more, again and again. I go to the river (the temple within) every morning on my walk and many times throughout my day. While there, I also visit with and sit with my light beings—I ask for their help, and I can feel them/sense them rushing to me. Later in the book the voice will explain that we all have a "deal" with our light beings …

Many people have written about the other side. I do not claim to be an expert on it, but the voice has informed me to a certain extent. It is known, in the ethereal realm, that being incarnated in the human realm is difficult. The voice tells us that before incarnating again, we have each decided—together with our light beings—whose turn it will be to incarnate this time around. It is now our turn. It has also been decided that our light beings will remain behind, to be with us at all times—in the ethereal, in our rivers—to help us. They have patiently waited for us to wake up and are thrilled that we can see them again.

I am getting ahead, but please don't abandon ship. The lessons that follow are deeper and more esoteric, but their value is priceless, as they lead us into a magnificent and brilliant new way of living in the here and now. A way in which we are fully grounded into the greater reality—connected to a pulse not of this planet—resonating at a higher frequency. Steeped in our highest selves. Living as our highest selves. Radiating. One. Naturally emanating our most spectacular symphony, and blooming our most vibrant colors.

By living in this greater reality, we raise our energy and change our own lives. And in so doing, we naturally influence the wavelength of the planet—*without focusing on an outcome of changing anyone or anything around us*. Humankind is at a juncture in the road. We are poised to awaken or not; to heal or not; to move beyond darkness—or not. As such, we each have the power within to tip the balance, contribute to the awakening of a new earth, and effect positive change across our planet, with light and healing overcoming shadow.

"And So It Is"

In the following lessons, the voice speaks to each of us directly and calls us to wake up. Change does not happen in the collective, he says. Change on the planet will naturally occur with one person at a time lighting up from within.

It is possible, and it is time.

14

"Home," the Temple of God, the River of Light, and the Light Beings

Lesson 57: This Is Real

And so it is ...

Nothing you see is Real.

Material things exist in the physical realm for you to see, to use, to live in, to work with, and to experience; but they are not "Real."

You must learn to look beyond, behind, and inside what you see—to seek the energy within an object—because that which presents on the obvious, physical level is not Real.

It is present, yes.

It is there, yes.

But it is material; it is the obvious; it is physical manifestation. What is Real cannot be readily seen with your human, conditioned eyes.

Behind and inside the material things in your physical dimension, that is where you will find what is Real.

"And So It Is"

What is Real—What do I mean by *Real*?

Real is pure energy, the All, the Divine, the Source of All things: *the elemental form of all things.* This is where I reside, where we souls that no longer dwell in physical incarnation reside.

It is all that is; it is what everything is made up of; it is the glue that binds us together as connected and one. It is a place you can envision in your mind, and it is accessible to you at all times.

It is a space within you—*it is the temple of God—it is home.*

When you are able to consciously live from this place within, you can create the life you want, and you will naturally uplift your energy. By uplifting your own energy, you will emit an energy unlike the wavelength of the planet. By emitting an accelerated energy, as you are, as you stand, as you live, as you reside in your life, you will naturally shine. When you shine, you are the light, and you can—without effort or conscious action—light another's candle: *You become the light the world so needs.*

You have the ability to change the way you see, what you know, and how you perceive the world around you. You have the ability to change yourself and the energy you emit, and in so doing, you can naturally ignite, illumine, uplift, and awaken a new earth.

It is time.

You cannot find *Real* by force, or by thinking hard with your mind. You find it by *releasing* yourself from mind and ego, and from shadow and darkness. For when you are standing in these things, you remain mired in the physical, and remain separate, living in the flat dimension of the material plane, residing in what *appears* Real, yet still disconnected.

Real is where the illusion of the material world dwells

not. It is a place you cannot fully comprehend but is somehow known and familiar. It is a place you are able to access within when you release yourself from seeing and experiencing only that which readily presents itself, and allow yourself to see from your essence: you access it by shifting your focus and seeing from the eyes of your soul.

This is not theoretical.

You have heard it said, "Change your mind, change your life," and that is true.

Step away from what you believe you know. Release yourself from mind and ego. Allow yourself to see the unseen, and to sense the unknown.

Most of your planet resides where physical illusion reigns supreme, seeking a plastic playland.

Dare to seek more.

When you release yourself from seeing only the physical, flat manifestation of the material world, you will no longer comprehend the world around you in the same way, nor will you experience life in the same way. You will accelerate, oscillate at a higher frequency, and begin to shift into a higher level of consciousness.

Stay grounded, be aware, and release into this shift within.

It is Real.

All that you see readily in the material plane is not Real. Look beyond it.

Seek to see with new eyes, the eyes of your soul.

"And So It Is"

Lesson 58: The Temple of God Within You

And so it is ...

The temple of God is Real and it is within you.

It is yours to come to, to reside in, and to experience.

You earn the ability to access it, and to live in it, by releasing yourself from what is unreal.

You earn the ability to access it, and to live in it, by stripping away all that blinds you from seeing.

You are invited.

Accept your invitation.

The temple of God is within you.

It exists beyond what you see readily.

It exists beyond where you are in physical form.

You access it, see it, enter it by letting go of mind, letting go of ego, letting go of the physical and of the habits of daily living. You will know when you have entered because:

All else falls away,

    You feel at home,

    You *are* home and you *understand*.

You comprehend that you are home—comprehending it in your cells, in your vessel.

You understand living on this earth but not being of it.

You become able to live in the beyond that is within you.

When you are able to do this, all will change for you, but at the same time, nothing will. You will continue to walk the same streets and drive in the same car—but you will do so differently. You will see with new eyes and live with wholeness within and strength abounding. You will be connected to something far greater than what you can explain. You will become One with the All.

There is no right or wrong time to arrive. There is no judgment. When your soul is ready, you will be ready.

You have your invitation.

Let go of mind.

Let go of ego.

The temple of God is within.

It is yours to come to, to experience, and to reside in.

It is yours to sit with the angels, and to be welcomed by the souls you know—and have known for eternity. Many have gone before you, and they await your arrival home. You need not leave your physical vessel to attain the temple of God within. You need not shift the space-time continuum. It is yours to come to, and to reside in, even while you remain in human form. When you find the temple within:

Your beauty increases,

Your light shines more radiantly,

Your joy is boundless,

Your contentment—profound.

Nothing you see with your physical eyes is Real, and that which is Real is beyond.

It is within.

And so it is.

"And So It Is"

Lesson 59: The Temple of God Surrounding You

And so it is ...
    The temple of God is also all around you.
    What you see readily, with your human eyes, is but a physical representation of energy.
    None of it is *Real*.
    What is Real is behind what you see.
    What is Real is above, below, and all around you, without presenting as matter, but as energy.
    It is invisible to the eyes you are accustomed to using, but it can be seen once you strip away what blinds you.
    What you see is what you will be.
    When what you see and feel and experience are limited to what obviously presents itself, you remain asleep.
    Awaken.
    Awaken to what exists beyond the material.
    Awaken to what is Real.
    Sink into that which matters.
    As you release what blinds you—the distractions before you, all around you, and even within you—you will be better able to pull back the curtain of separation. When you remove this curtain you will step forward onto a new pathway. It is illumined. It is yours to tread in order to place your life on a new trajectory, where you are one with pure

beauty, truth, power, and dignity, able to transcend the reality of human living and to co-create.

Here, there is no lack.

Here, there is no shadow.

Here, you are free.

When you step away from the false sense of security of mind and ego and strip away what binds you to earthly reality, you will soar.

When you see, then so shall you be.

Allow yourself to see.

The temple of God is all around you. With each step you take, you are moving within the temple of God. Each street you walk upon, each particle of air you breathe; it all emanates from the temple of God.

So there you are.

Surrounded entirely by the temple of God.

It is within you. It is around you. It is All.

It is within you.

It is around you.

All. It is All. There is naught but this.

Source it. Step consciously into it.

As you are, as you see, so shall you be.

The only separation is in your mind.

"And So It Is"

Lesson 60: The River of Light and the Light Beings

And so it is …

In the temple you can sense the All. You can see your guides. You are in, and of, and surrounded by the river of light. See it. Sense it. It is clean, bright, warm, and wet, but it is not like the water on earth. It is light: radiant light. The river is of a healing, divine nature—it is the Source of All, the well of power, the brilliant fountain of pure light and love. You can come here for cleansing and renewal and connection at any time of the day or night. You can carry yourself from this sacred place within as you walk through every step of your day.

In the temple there are also other souls present and surrounding you; we shall call them *light beings*. They have awaited your arrival and your return home. Allow yourself to see them. Allow them to greet you, and allow them to give you their love.

When you come to the temple regularly, all things are made new.

You will shine. You will radiate.

You will strengthen.

You will be able to join with pure thought.

You will become as light.

Breathe in, focus, and live from *this* place.

This is the only Real.

The other is but illusion.
You want to change your life: change your mind.
Change it by getting out of it and away from it.
The new is not more of the same.
To change, you must change.
To change, you must see differently.
That which you see is how you will be.
Come to the temple within.
It is light, and it is within you, and all around you.
It is All.
It is everything.
Nothing you see readily is Real.
See more.

Seek what is Real. Come to the temple within. You can live in it with eyes that can see it, awareness that can know it, and power that emanates from it.

The physical world is but illusion.

Lesson 61: Play in the River

And so it is ...

Come home.

Come to the temple within.

See yourself here.

See the light beings all around you.

See the energy of that which is Real. See the river of flowing light around you: white-gold in color, radiating, bright, warm. Feel its power.

Stand in the river. Cup the light, the water, the purest of pure elements and drip it over your head, stroke it upon your face and body, lather yourself in it, drink of it so you are renewed and cleansed.

A-a-a-ah. You are drawn to play in it, to splash, to delight in it, to become childlike and joyful within, expressing pure happiness and deep, gleeful joy. Play! Splash! Laugh! You are a child at home, feeling the bliss of no worries, the knowledge that it is safe here, that here is where you are filled and become complete, and that from here you can go out and face another day in the world of the material.

Come here. Come home. Live from here. Live in here. And when you become entangled with what is unreal, simply return to this place to be renewed and strengthened.

This is the temple of God. It is within you.

You have found home.

"Home"

You have completed the circle.
The merging is realized.
You will now accelerate.
From here your work and your fun begin!

Lesson 62: In the Temple, There Is Peace

And so it is ...
>Beauty surrounds.
>Light enthralls.
>Allow this moment to envelop you.
>See me; I am all around.
>Feel me; I am here.
>Hear me; I am the angelic voice of the quiet.
>Know this peace.
>Feel this peace.
>Be this peace.
>Live from this peace.
>Sense the wonder.
>Allow this moment to envelop you.
>Try not to go from this place.
>But know that when you do, it remains here, awaiting your return.
>Surrounding you.
>Supporting you.
>Guiding you home.

Lesson 63: In the Temple, There Is Renewal

And so it is …

Come to the temple: the center of your being, where All is and where Real is.

From here you are one with truth, beauty, pure knowledge, and light.

From here you reside physically on your earth, but one with the consciousness of All.

From here you become renewed.

From here you can place yourself in light at all times, so you are not depleted during your day but walk full, whole, and complete.

From here you know peace, love, true connection, and even blissful joy.

When you come here, you are renewed.

This is home, your center, your core.

Home.

As you see, so shall you be.

As you see home, feel home, and *are home*, you become capable of more.

The illusion is that you have control in your physical world, that you are capable of shifting and leading situations to your desired outcome. Sometimes it works—more often, not. The distraction is your futile attempt to continue the illusion.

"And So It Is"

To have, hold onto, and be in Real power, let go of all control.

Let go of attempts at control.

Let go of illusion.

And focus on living from this place within—home—the temple within.

Your power is here.

From here you are renewed.

Lesson 64: See the Real

And so it is ...
    Behind all you see lies what is Real.
    Within all you feel lies what is true.
    Around you at all times lies what is pure.
    When you see it not, it is because you are distracted: your mind has gone to chatter and occupies too much space within your vessel.
    Cleanse yourself of shadow within.
    Rid yourself of distraction within.
    Ground yourself to what is Real within.
    Find your way home to the temple within you.
    Breathe from here.
    Stand in this power.
    Straighten your spine.
    Lift up your chin.
    Raise up your eyes, and see from here.
    As you see, so shall you be.

Lesson 65: The Temple and the River Are *All* and *Everything*

And so it is ...

As you come to the temple, you find solace.

As you stay in the temple, you change.

Your Real power comes from the temple.

The temple is where all things become manifest.

The light, the river, the light beings—they are all here for you.

This place is Real.

This place is within you.

Place: this is a word we use to orient to location, but in reality the temple of God is everywhere. You source it today from within, but soon you will see that there is naught but this temple.

You live in the temple physically, although you cannot see it.

You can sense it at times, when ego and mind are set aside.

When you quiet within and allow distractions to slip away, you can feel its boundless power, perfect presence, and absolute and all-encompassing unity and light.

You will not see it with your human eyes, but you will know it by seeing with your essence and with the eyes of your soul.

Go within. Place yourself in the temple, and as you

look around you, the physical world will appear different to you; the energy behind what you are able to see with your human eyes bleeds through; the energy around all living things shimmers.

You know you are part of what is beyond.

You feel you have transformed from one-dimensional living to sensing and resonating with the All.

Place yourself here as often as you can.

Live from this place for as much of the time as you can, readily aware of being one with the All, the river of light, and the light beings.

You know you have arrived when you feel complete, full, round, and whole.

Breathe this in.

Sit in this place.

Reside in this place.

Push not.

Force not.

Simply allow yourself to release into this place, and with that release, become more …

Here you can heal.

Here you can find comfort.

Here are your light beings.

Here are your guides.

Here you find connection to what is Real and true.

Here you can create.

Here is power: what you *envision* here, you can manifest.

Here is energy: what you *shape* here, you can have.

Here is love: what you *are* here transcends human emotion and life.

Here, you grow and transform and awaken.

You need not push or force.

You need not *do* anything when you are here.

"And So It Is"

When you come here, you are one with All.

Lie down in this energy.

Sink down into the river of light. Allow it to wash over and through you, and become one with you.

When you come here, you are renewed and strengthened.

When you come here repeatedly, your life will be changed.

Lesson 66: Come to the River

And so it is ...

Come to the river.
Here is your home.
Come to the river.
Here is the temple within.
Come to the river.
Here is where you find peace, comfort, strength, and the energy of the All.
Come to the river.
Here is within you.
Come to the river.
Here is what you find when you rid yourself of all distractions, mind, and ego.
Come to the river.
Take my hand—I will lead you.
Come to the river.
This is unlike other rivers.
This river is light. It is made up of light. It flows ... but not like water.
It is liquid but thicker than water.
It is tepid, but you do not feel it.
It is light beings.
It is the All.
It is here; it is Real.
Come to the river.

"And So It Is"

Step into the shallows at its edge.

Come to the river—though you see it as a river flowing on the ground, look again.

See the river.

It surrounds you.

It is above, below, beside you, but it is still a river.

Stand in it. Sit down in it. Strip away the clothing you wear that separates you from feeling the river water, the light water on your vessel.

Lie down in it.

Swim in it.

Drink of it.

Luxuriate in the river.

It is home.

Here, you are one with All.

As you look around at the earthly world where you reside, do so from the vantage of the river.

See the river.

Get into the river.

Feel the light beings that are in and of the river. You are one with them.

Here you find light, love, pure thought, knowledge, truth, and beauty.

Here you are renewed.

Here you are one with everything that is, has been, and ever will be.

Get into the river.

Swim in the river, in this light, with these light beings. See yourself flowing along, stroking through the water.

Swim.

Understand and see that there is no separation between you and the river.

You swim as a mermaid.

You swim as a drop of this water of light.
You are the river.
You are this energy.
You are this light.
You are the All.
You are me.
Here, we are one.
All is energy.
All flows from this light.
Come to the river.
Here you are changed, healed, transformed.

Here you can release into all that your birthright holds for you: light, truth, dignity, power, strength, abundance, love, joy, peace, oneness with All, fullness, wholeness, completeness.

Strip away any distractions, any residual remnants of thought telling you that lacking is normal, that you are unworthy, that it is shallow and selfish to ask for money and financial security. *Strip these thoughts away.* Receive fullness and completion. When you are abundant—secure in yourself, your worth, and yes, even secure in your bank account—you fret and worry not.

Let yourself be filled.

Let yourself receive abundance. Financial security is not bad. You are not less spiritual to ask for this.

Come to the temple.
Come to the river.
Free yourself of darkness.
Free yourself of distractions.
Come to the river.
Lay down your garments.
Step into the river.
Sit down in the river.

"And So It Is"

Lie down in the river. Let the light beings carry you, hold you, swim with you, caress and heal you.

Swim with them.

Let go of your fear, and your overthinking and analysis.

Be in the river.

Swim.

Swim until you swim like a mermaid.

Swim until you swim as one with me, the river, and the light beings.

Swim as a mermaid, and see, and know in that moment of awareness:

You are the river, you are a light being, and you are this—the All. You are one with the All: with All that is, that has been, that ever will be. You are one. You are this energy. You are this light. You are the All.

Come to the river.

And from here, from this place, you can create.

From here, from this place, you can receive.

Come to the river.

From this place, you receive, give, receive and give, receive, give. As you are able to accept, as your vessel strengthens, as your sense of self grows, you can more readily step forward into the All. Then more can be poured into you, and you receive more, give more, receive more, give more, and continue the circle, helping others.

Come to the river.

Be filled from here. Grow in completeness and fullness in all ways and all things.

Come to the river.

It is the Source of All.

Come to the river.

Notes

15

Living in the World

Lessons 67 through 72 are a series of lessons that arrived during a tumultuous time in our world: a worldwide pandemic was sweeping over our planet; forest fires had erupted across the continents; racial divides intensified, escalated, and flared into dangerous conflict; politics grew even more polarized; and opposition to those *unlike us* ran rampant and deep.

In this series of lessons, the voice provides us with perspective and guidance, utilizing the universal truths he explained in the prior section to help us navigate through times of chaos and unrest such as these. The voice invites us to resonate at the highest frequency we are capable of during each moment at hand. He tells us that when we do the things he teaches, we are able to live in sync with the power of the All. And while we do not directly tackle the issues of the planet and of humankind, we naturally influence the waves of energy of which everything is made. Without *focusing on* outcomes, we *positively influence* outcomes.

This is contagious, he tells us.

We learn to seek change for no one else but for our own soul, so that as we are, as we stand, as we live, as we reside in our life, we shine. We transmute as light and, without effort or conscious

"And So It Is"

action, naturally light another's candle, tipping the balance and effecting positive change across our planet.

The more we maintain uplifted energy, the more of a difference we can make. The voice tells us not to allow dark news, the dark behavior of others, fears within and without, or the surrounding chaos to influence our way of being. This is not always easy—but we always have a choice.

Lesson 67: Fear Not and Focus on You

And so it is ...

Worry not.

Worry not about where this is going, where you will end up, where these lessons are taking you, what the exterior world is becoming, why the leaders of your nations behave as they do, how it seems so mucked up, how much you wish it to be different. Worry not on this; obsess not on this. You cannot control this. Pay attention, yes. Obsess, no.

You must focus on what is yours to control: yourself, your thoughts, and your actions. Be not swayed by what happens around you. Be not controlled by the darkness your world presents. Yes, it is out of control. Yes, it flies against your comfort zone. Do not deny its existence, but if you become obsessed with these things outside yourself, you will become sick, weakened in spirit, ungrounded, afraid, and reactive. The world cannot handle more reactivity.

Be grounded.

Set yourself firmly on the ground, planted in your feet, drawing strength from the earth and power and might from its ever-churning core. Connect to that which is Real, that which is unseen but there: the energy and strength of the All, the power of the divine, the temple within.

One way or another, this all will end. How is not yet clear. But you are still here, strong, light filled, radiant,

"And So It Is"

brimming with Real power. Set in your mind that these are the things to place your focus on.

Look not at the unknowns, and do not ponder each possible turn of events.

Fear not about upcoming elections and the future of political powers.

Stray not from setting your mind and your day on living in strength, light, love, power, wholeness, fullness, and completeness, and on your own path of light. Live by focusing on these things, regardless of the circumstances around you.

Some days it is easier to do this, some days harder.

On those days when it is easier, be grateful. On those days when it is harder, separate yourself from fear. Remain aware when chatter, anxiety, or darkness circles in wild thoughts in your head—and stop. Get out of your head and away from the chatter, and come back to your feet. Surround yourself in light. Stop the racking mind and racing heart. Breathe. Come to the temple within.

There will be days like this.

There are people on your planet who live to create this darkness and chaos. This is true; you do not imagine it. And you cannot control them.

You can control yourself.

You are unaware of the impact you have when you refuse angst and refuse to let darkness permeate your soul. Your comprehension matters not. What matters is your complete dedication and unwavering commitment to standing firmly planted, grounded in light, strong and whole, full and complete.

This is contagious.

Focus not on what is outside you, on the circumstances of others.

Focus on yourself: Your feet planted. Your back straight. Chin up, eyes up, breathing love in and out, connected to pure truth and Real power. Radiating.

This is how you drive change in your life.

This is how you drive change on your planet.

This is how you calm the storms of hate, violence, anger, racism, vicious attacks. Do not stray from this place.

As you think of your leaders, those making decisions affecting the whole world, and as you think of people in general—from this place only—greet them using your thoughts. Surround them with this energy, lift them up, and send them a ball of pure white light energy. Throw it at them as you would a snowball. It will dissolve onto them and around them.

When enough people remain calm, clear, one with All, firmly planted, seeing and seeking only Real power, the axis can tilt. *But seek not to tilt the axis.* Worry not about outcomes. They are not yours to control. Just stay put where you are planted, in your feet, emanating, reflecting, being, and acting from light and Real strength.

"And So It Is"

Lesson 68: Trust in Awareness

And so it is ...
    The peace you feel within is Real.
    The fullness you feel within is Real.
    The fear, worry, angst, and anxiousness you sometimes feel within are not Real. They arrive when you are not connected to what is Real.
    It is not bad when this happens.
    And you have not failed.
    You are still human, and incapable of continually remaining connected. You will still go to these places in your mind—but hopefully less frequently than you used to, and for a shorter time when you do.
    In your journey, you have begun to awaken.
    In your awakening, you have found greater awareness.
    In your awareness, you have begun to recognize when you are falling away from what is Real.
    Awareness means you can again center and connect:
    Immediately move from head into feet.
    Immediately source light.
    Immediately place yourself in the temple.
    Breathe in from here.
    Release yourself from your shadow thoughts.
    Allow yourself to be restored.

Allow yourself to be renewed.

Allow yourself to feel the depth of your connection to the All.

Breathe in. Breathe out.

"And So It Is"

Lesson 69: Cool the Flames

And so it is ...

You know how to send a snowball of white light energy from your mind to another: You picture the person or the place you intend to receive the energy. You picture the snowball, and place whatever it is you wish to send into it. Then you throw the ball with your mind.

Send wisdom, truth, healing, peace, calm thoughts, and sensible reason to your leaders. The energy you send will flow onto them and be absorbed by them.

Picture a map of the world in your mind. You can see energetic blotches on this map, areas that are red, hot, and erupting. Send cooling snowballs of peace, healing, and light to these areas of your planet.

Your world is not calm.

Fear prevails.

Hatred, prejudice, darkness, lies, posturing, self-protection, and the brink of war are looming. Send healing snowballs. Do not fall to fear. Get back in your feet. Fill yourself with light, stand strong, stand one, and stand tall. Hold yourself in Real power, dignity, peace, wholeness, and fullness. See and know:

As you see, so shall you be.

As you radiate, so you are.

Gather the energy ball in your mind again. Into it, intend peace to calm the waves of unrest, water to soothe

the fires of hate and the burning of your planet, healing energy to mitigate disease, and rational thinking to fill your leaders and all your people. Then, throw it.

See this.

Stand in this.

Hold this possibility.

Do not let yourself move to fear. Do not allow the energy sweeping your planet to consume you.

Lesson 70: Keep Your Footing

And so it is ...

The energy on your planet is, how shall we say it? Not peaceful.

Nations are at war.

Politicians are scheming.

Citizens are afraid.

Do not become confused or caught up in these times and these threats.

Stay grounded, and at peace within. Purposefully stand in your feet, and do not fall into the rapids of emotion and fear. Stay out of your head, and stay out of worry, for if you succumb to these, you will lose yourself.

Your world leaders are at a tipping point.

That which you see has been prescribed.

This does not make it easier to see, but with that knowing, stay planted so you do not lose your footing.

When you become afraid, calm yourself and send your leaders a snowball of peace.

Lesson 71: Seek Light

And so it is ...
    You ask: What will become of us?
    You will either awaken or you will not.
    Many of your people are in shadow.
    Many of your people are finding it easy to embrace dark power: blame, hatred, jealousy, negative talk, hurt. Many are purposefully embracing lower-level emotions to elevate their own sense of self and their power over others, rather than doing the work of looking at their actual selves and the energy *they* project.
    Do not focus on this.
    Do not allow this into your being.
    And do not consider this direction to be either futile or too simplistic.
    As you see, so shall you be.
    You need not fall into this perspective of living. Your worldview ought not be dictated by the dark behaviors of others. When you notice it affecting you, step away. Come to the temple within. Fill with light. Breathe from here, and do not let encroaching darkness enter your being or touch your soul.
    Soul work is sometimes about protection.
    Soul seeks light.

"And So It Is"

Soul blossoms with light and withers without it.
Seek light.
Stay apart from that which kills.

Lesson 72: Continue Your Inward Journey

And so it is ...

The journey is an inward one.

To change the outer world, change your inner world.

To change your inner world, quiet the mind: focus on that which is Real—though unseen. Focus on that which matters—yet is not readily apparent. Focus on that which you can control—though it is not what it appears to be.

As the outer world swarms with chaotic energy, fear, and unknown outcomes, allow yourself peace. Let the angst fall away. You watch the news, the political games, the machinations and lies, and they permeate your being. You become consumed by the disorder, unable to quiet the mind and unable to still within. Not only do you need to access the temple within you; you must also pay heed to what you surround yourself with. Receive too much of the dark news and you will fall to unrest.

When you feel or think I have left you, know this: I will never leave you. If you cannot find me, if you cannot locate the temple within, if you cannot source the light or meet the light beings, know that you have created a shadow wall between us—built of day-to-day distractions that have piled up. Watch the wall carefully as it begins to rise. Knock it down quickly and come back to what is soulful, light, Real; come back to what matters. Yes, the state of your world matters, war matters, but *you will not change the energy of war by standing in the energy of war.* Step out, step aside. Remain separate from the dark games that fly about, and center yourself.

As you see, so shall you be.

As you are, then can you bring more light.

Remember who you really are.

Remember what you really are.

Remember what is Real.

Focus on what is Real, though unseen.

Focus on what matters, though it is not readily apparent.

Focus on what you can control, though it is not what it appears to be.

Notes

16

Come Within

Lesson 73: Live from the Temple Within

In the next couple of lessons the voice places his focus again on us: on our days, our mindsets, and where to place our attention, rather than the larger and broader topics he has recently introduced. I believe he steps away purposefully in order to remind us to consciously manage and maintain a right mindset in our day-to-day living. Later he describes this back and forth as a means of giving us a break from the more "heady" and esoteric messages. Each of the lessons is presented in the book in the same order as it arrived—meaning the voice delivered his lessons in this back-and-forth manner. Perhaps he offers heady, esoteric, and political lessons and then gives us a break from them, as a hint at how to manage through life: taking a break from thinking about and working with the "big stuff" is sometimes just what we need. Later he tells us not to seek the other side too fervently, that we might miss the wonder of living this incarnation. *Live the illusion! Dream the dream! Enjoy the ride!* he says, for we have chosen to incarnate again in order to experience living as a human on earth.

"And So It Is"

Yes, perhaps a break is sometimes warranted, indeed.

But back to Lesson 73 …

We all have days when everything seems *"just right,"* days that are often described as *good-hair days.*

Perhaps we woke up to a sunshiny day, maybe a low-pressure system has lifted, or perhaps it is a day we have looked forward to that has finally arrived. Regardless, there are days when we feel good and confident and we radiate from within. These are days when we naturally walk tall and smile without forcing. People we meet on our way *"see"* us, and it feels like they are drawn to us. We feel good about ourselves, and it shows. We all have these days, and they are great days.

Toward the end of this next lesson, the voice describes this sort of day in better detail: Rather than empty, we know full. Rather than fearful, we are at peace. Rather than shadow, we radiate light … We claim pure ease. The world around us falls into place, not because we have attempted to force it all into place—it is just a day like this.

He goes on to say *how* this happens: *it happens when we do not place our focus on what is outside us.* It happens when we step outside of neediness. It happens when we come within, connect to what is Real, and maintain our connection to the temple within.

This is an extremely important reminder: We must do the things that *set our day* to be good. *We* are in charge of the type of day we have. Even on those days when we know we're not having a good-hair day, or when chaos swirls, we can still set our day to be good. We do not need the stuff around us to be good in order for the day to be good; a day is good when we put ourselves in the place to make it so.

When we are ready, we learn to come within—to the temple within—where our best self and truth reside, and where we interact with our light beings and become renewed. When we are ready, we learn to seek only what is Real; live in this moment only; let thoughts of all else fall away; and seek not from any event outside ourselves to determine the course of our day. *Then* we step bravely, majestically, and boldly—and live brilliantly in our radiant and blossoming life.

In this lesson the voice also discusses the treasure chest we all have within us.

I remember the first time he began talking about the treasure chest, and how he uses the image *"throw open the lid of the treasure chest within you."* It is a vivid picture. It is not difficult to see a treasure chest with the lock removed, lid laid back fully, and the treasure spilling over out of the top, falling into glorious piles all around. *That which is spilling over is all the gifts we have kept locked up tight.* The gifts we have not allowed ourselves to receive—perhaps from feeling unworthy, perhaps from claiming a mindset of lack. We will be invited later to examine why we have repelled this receiving, but hopefully by now we feel more worthy and are more ready and able to receive. A good day is ours to claim. The gifts the universe has in mind for us are ours to claim too. The voice invites us to throw open the lid! Claim our destiny! Live our true purpose! Release into our true being and our radiant life, assuring us that from this place of oneness and sureness, our path forward brilliantly unfolds.

We can set our day.

We can throw open the lid—and receive.

Come within.

In this context, how silly it seems that we would allow our minds to run amok, ruminating on yesterday (over) or fretting about tomorrow (not yet here).

In this moment, in this *now* is your life.

As you see, so shall you be.

Today is a new day. Choose wisely.

"And So It Is"

❖

And so it is ...
    You come within and find yourself.
    You come within and find truth.
    Seek not outside yourself.
    Seek only what is Real.
    Fear not the future.
    Live in *this* moment and let thoughts of all else fall away.
    Yesterday: gone.
    Tomorrow: not yet here.

In this moment, in this *now*, is your life. Tomorrow will be governed by the connection you build to what is Real today. Tomorrow will be dictated by the paths your feet tread today and your comprehension of *As you see, so shall you be*.

In this moment, focus on walking your illumined path. Step bravely, majestically, knowing that you are one with All, your life is destined, and your job is to step forward into what has been chosen for you: light, truth, dignity, power, strength, abundance, love, joy, peace, oneness with All, fullness, wholeness, completeness.

Throw open the lid of the treasure chest within you to claim your destiny and live your true purpose. Release into your true being and your radiant life. From this place of oneness and sureness, your path forward unfolds.

Come within for healing, recharging, revealing, and reconnecting.

And as you walk through your day mindful of and consciously aware of the temple within, see how differently you observe what is around you:

Rather than empty, you know full.
Rather than fear, you are peace.

Rather than shadow, you radiate light.

Rather than experiencing people you encounter as bothersome, in your way, you claim pure ease. The outside world falls into place, not because you have placed your focus on changing what is outside you but because you have stepped aside from doing that, as you are operating from the temple within. You are in flow. You are one. You are whole and complete, and today all is well.

This.

This, my dear, is how you set today to be a good day.

Fret not.

Live from the temple within today.

Lesson 74: You Are Becoming, and This Is Real

And so it is ...
    You are part of the All.
    You are one of the many.
    You are a drop of the All.
    You *are* the All.
    We are all one.
    One river.
    One being.
    One celestial light force.
    You are a drop of the river.
    You are a ray of the light.
    As you see, so shall you be.
    You see your part of the All in the All.
    You see what being one really is.
    You see that your vessel is but your vessel—and that your spirit is who you really are.
    You see that you, too, are a light being and a drop of the river of light—*but you are also the whole river.*
    You see that the temple of God is within you, and is accessible to you at any time. And whether you are consciously aware of the temple in a particular moment, you know that you live in the temple at all times.
    We are all one.
    Step confidently.

You are becoming.
This is Real.
Smile.

This lesson overflows with absolute beauty and pure truth.

When I feel alone and disconnected, I find this is a good lesson to read again. Perhaps you will be drawn to it at such times too.

"And So It Is"

Lesson 75: Accept Yourself with Tenderness

And so it is ...

You grow and then your soul rests for a bit.

You grow some more and then your soul rests for a bit.

This is how it goes, this becoming.

There is never a straight trajectory on this nonstop flight toward change.

That would be too much—you need to rest in between.

As you grow, layers peel away and the nuances of situations appear to you. New perspectives on yourself can arise if you use eyes of tenderness, acceptance, and love.

Hold the person you once were with love. Let that person know you accept and love them fully as they once were. For now you know: the person you are today did not emerge in spite of yesterday—but because of it. Do not shame yourself for anything. Understand that, yes, today if you were presented with the same situations, you would make different choices. But yesterday, you tried. You did the best you could do. All you had to give, you gave. So let go of retrying the case, of revisiting situations of the past. Send love, peace, acceptance, and even gratitude to your former self for making it through, despite wishing now that things had unfolded differently.

Healing? Yes, you are.

Growing? Yes, you are.

Loving? Yes, you are learning to love not only the positive and easy parts of yourself but those parts of you (and of others) that were in shadow, and sometimes are even today.

Accept self, even the self of yesterday.

Be tender with your soul.

It matters.

"And So It Is"

Lesson 76: Reconcile with Your Higher Self

In the last lesson we were reminded that we grow and then our soul rests for a bit. We grow some more and then our soul rests for a bit, again. That this is how it goes, this becoming: we are never on a straight trajectory on a nonstop flight toward change. That would be too much.

Again, he has given us a break between the more heady, esoteric, and universal truth lessons in this book. Next he dives back in ...

Enjoy.

And a special note: *Many of these concepts the voice shares are not "new."*

You may observe that the voice delivers universal truths that many of us have encountered before in various forms, passed down in writings and teachings through the ages. The difference for me has been that he casts these truths in his own, distinctive way—and with loving support—*with the aim of teaching us how to utilize them* to heal the scars we have carried on our souls, to enhance and uplift our lives, and to live in such a way that we can help awaken ourselves to a new world.

In this lesson, he begins to describe everything as energy and says that we will learn, over time, how to shape it. While we see, for example, a tree, and we know it to be *tree*, it is really pure energy oscillating into tree form.

The street below our feet is not just a street: it is really pure energy becoming and displaying the visual and physical manifestation of *street*. He reminds us again that our human eyes cannot see this, but that our essence knows. He is inviting us to go deeper. He is inspiring us to allow ourselves to see more and seek more.

When we are able to do this, we learn to live in a way in which we straddle both worlds—the physical world and the *middle world*.

Our ability to connect to the middle world is a necessary step to being able to source Real power.

Our challenge is to practice so we become more adept at doing this each day.

We have often heard the word *reconcile*, and from this word, this lesson begins.

When we incarnate, we do so as beautiful, shiny, bouncing babies. It has been said that babies sleep so much because they are still intimately connected to the ethereal, and their napping is their direct conduit to "home." They can still hear the angels singing; that is how closely they are connected to the other side. When we age, we lose this connection—and we forget. We lose the memory of the ethereal, and we lose conscious awareness of our Higher Selves so we can begin living as fully human and grounded in this physical plane.

The voice explains it simply: As we aged from infancy, we lost our awakening and became separated from awareness. While our Higher Self always remained with us, we forgot it. *Our purpose now is to reconcile*—that we will remember who we really are, capable of sourcing our Real life force.

We are here, at this time, for a reason.

You, I, all of us who are interested are called to awaken and reconcile. It makes sense that in this lesson, the voice tells us, *"The reconciling and the awakening on your planet are actually speeding along, but you doubt that because the darkness is so loud right now. The louder the clatter of the darkness, the more committed you must become to reconciling."*

We are alive at a powerful time. Humankind is at a juncture in the road, and we are poised to either awaken or not. While we cannot control the awakening of other people, we *can* control ourselves, and the voice invites us to continue to meld further into the ethereal while we are incarnated on earth.

Along the way, he tells us, we will meet those who are like us, further igniting the collective spark. As more of us awaken and reconcile, while the clatter will get louder for a time, fewer and fewer people will be left to hear the noise.

This lesson inspires us to create our day so that what we hear most predominantly is the beautiful quiet of peace, and the pure and true sound of the ethereal.

And so it is ...

We come to a new level of your becoming.

Our new word is *reconcile*.

When you incarnated into the world, you did so in order to experience being human, your soul being ready for another journey through the human endeavor.

Your soul came here to experience life as a human being rather than as a pure spirit. The wheels were set in motion. And when you incarnated, you lost your awakening. You became separated from your awareness of your Higher Self and your connection to the All.

Your Higher Self remained with you, but your human self and mind were unaware.

On your life journey, your purpose is to reconcile with your Higher Self.

When you reconcile, you remember who you really are and you step into Real power—your Real life force. You become able to transcend daily situations and circumstances and see beyond them. You are conscious of living as a human being, on this earth but not of it.

Your beauty shines,
Your abundance soars,
Your joy is boundless,
Your fear diminished,
Your power consolidated,
Your radiance bright,
Your peace magnified,
Your resourcefulness at your fingertips,
Your worry gone.

You become one with "creator mode." You can hold the energy of all things in your hands. You may not see the vibrating energy of the material world around you, but you understand and know that the tree that presents in front of you is really pure energy oscillating into tree form. The street below your feet is really pure energy becoming the visual and physical manifestation of the street. Deep within you, on the level where pure consciousness and deep comprehension reside, you know that the street you walk upon is the shimmering, glimmering radiant light of the I Am, the energy of All, and that it merges with the energy of you. Your human eyes cannot see this, but your essence knows.

As you reconnect, as you reconcile, you are better able to see and comprehend this. And then … then you can bring real change to your life.

As you see, so shall you be.
We have said this to you before.
See what you do not see.
Be what you do not see.
Live in what you do not see.
See the energy of all things.
Feel the energy of all things.
Reach your hands out in front of you and hold this

"And So It Is"

energy—unseen to your human eyes, but there. And as you hold it, envision in it that which you desire.

As you see, so shall you be.

See more.

Seek more.

See beyond.

Be not limited by what is readily apparent. It is there, but so too is what is behind it, inside it, of it: Me. Energy. Pure truth. None of the material world you readily see is Real.

You are straddling both worlds—the physical world and the middle world.

The reconciling and the awakening on your planet are actually speeding along, but you doubt that because the darkness is so loud right now.

The louder the clatter of the darkness, the more committed you must become to reconciling.

Do not try to comprehend; do not worry about comprehending.

Just continue to meld further into the ethereal while you are incarnated on earth. This is your purpose, your destiny, and as you further become and reconcile, so will you recognize others who are doing the same reconciling and walking a journey like yours.

As more people reconcile, the clatter will get louder—for a time. But as fewer and fewer hear the noise, the beautiful quiet of peace, the pure, the true will increase and surround you more fully.

Let the clatter go. Quiet the clatter by not paying it heed.

The step we take now is reconciling.

Notes

17

The Energy of the All

Lesson 77: The All Wishes to Rise

This is a pinnacle lesson.

When we fully reconcile, the voice says, it will mean many things: We will be able to see in a new way. Gifts will be revealed as never before. Our full potential will be easier to step into and realize. And yes, we will merge deeper with the ethereal while we remain living in human form during this incarnation on earth.

In this lesson, the voice teaches us how to merge into—how to *step* into—and how to stand in, and live from, the energy of the All. To do this, we must first comprehend that *everything is energy,* and secondly his words *"The All wishes to rise."*

Whatever does that mean?

It means this: Visualizing the "All" rising from the ground beneath our feet as pure energy (like a rising wave from a large body of water), and then visualizing ourselves becoming as pure energy, and merging into and standing—as pure energy ourselves—in, and as, part of the pure energy of the All.

To be able to comprehend this and do this, again we must be

"And So It Is"

able to envision the world around ourselves as pure energy—and to see it as such. I practiced and worked with this for many, many mornings as I walked. At first I glimpsed the energy shimmering around an object I passed by. Over time, I learned to do as the voice teaches in this lesson: I envisioned the path beneath my feet becoming pure energy, and then my vessel becoming pure energy. I was able to envision the path literally rising in its presentation as pure energy, and first my feet, and then my calves, and pretty soon my whole body wading into the energy of the path beneath me—as if I were wading into a river.

Initially, we are separate from what we are wading into. Then, we become as one.

In this lesson the voice also connects this exercise to the river. Earlier he stated that the temple of God (the river) is within us and all around us. Now, he clearly states that the "All" that rises, and that we step into, is like stepping into the river (the temple within) and that we are always in this river. This image inspires us to comprehend this truth in yet another way.

Now the voice's own words ...

And so it is ...

The reconciling of your human self with your Higher Self will mean many things. Your eyes will be opened to see in a new way. Your gifts will be revealed as never before. Your capacity will expand so that as you see more clearly, and receive greater awareness of your gifts, your capacity to realize your full potential will grow. You will fill with more light and merge deeper with the ethereal while walking on earth.

As you reconcile, you become.

As you reconcile, you can breathe more deeply, and in the quiet you are able to *see*.

As you see, so shall you be.

When you have looked around at the trees, the houses, the cars, the path beneath your feet, you have strained to see with your human eyes the energy that lies behind all physical reality. As you reconcile more fully with your Higher Self, you become aware that the word *see* has deeper meaning. Perhaps you cannot yet literally see the energy behind all things, but you will see the essence of this energy. And as you do this more regularly, your ability to see will increase.

Look at the path beneath your feet. It radiates. Feel the light. See the light, both below you and ahead of you. Step forward, knowing that this earth, this sacred ground radiates pure energy. See your feet: they too are pure energy—that is what *you* are. As you reconcile with your Higher Self, you are drawn to your center, where you know Real truth. Stay here, and from this place of connection, look out with your essence. You can see your feet merging into the path, the energy of your feet one with the energy of the path, and in that moment *you know that you are this same energy.*

All is one.

All is connected.

The energy of the path blends into your physical body, and it is like wading into a river.

You are in the river.

At all times, in all ways.

You and all things are one, made up of the same energy stuff, discerned in physical form by the human eye through the rapid oscillation of this energy. Tree energy oscillates into trees. All of the physical world is this vibrating energy.

"And So It Is"

As you see, so shall you be.

We spoke earlier of the hierarchy of souls.

Not all souls see as you see.

No problem.

Not all souls want to see as you see.

No problem.

Not all souls see only what you see—some see and know more.

No problem.

There is a continuum of souls on the path to illumination you are on. There is a continuum of awakening.

Many have gone before you.

Many will come behind you.

Some will wait and do it in another lifetime.

No problem.

Be who *you* are.

Remember who you are.

Embrace and accept where you are on the continuum, and do not berate yourself, no matter where you are.

Awaken to the eyes of the soul you have today.

Be here.

Stand here. Strong, whole, complete, full. Look about with your "understanding from within" eyes. See the path; see its energy. See the world in which you reside. Step forward and become one with all the energy surrounding you. This is just like stepping into the river in the temple. This is all there is; there is nothing else. You are always in the river, wading in it, swimming in it. The energy of the All is always around you—you're just not always awake enough to realize that nothing you see with your human eyes is what truly is. Energy is what truly is.

Your energy and the energy of your surroundings are the

same. You are one. You are part of everything, connected, like a drop in the river that is all there is.

As you see, so shall you be.

Now you know why there is no lacking in the I Am. The I Am just "is." As you come to live in this manner, placing yourself here in your mind's eye, you will further reconcile. You will increasingly live on this earth but not of it because you will know that what your human eye can see is not Real. You cannot be part of a mirage. You are Real. You and I are one. And as you further reconcile, you will understand that you walk on sacred ground—because the ground *is* the I Am, the All. You know there is no lack in the I Am; there cannot be. You will push through that delusional fear because it is but shadow.

You cannot have light without dark, up without down, high without low. But you can choose which of these opposites to reside within.

Choose light.

Be light.

Choose to reside in that which is Real. Walk on your path and allow *it* to rise up. Recall that many lessons ago we asked you to rise up and see—to really see from *here*.

The All wishes to rise.

The All wishes to present.

Allow the energy of the physical world to rise up so you can see it and step into it, knowing you are the same energy. You are one.

As the path beneath you rises as pure energy, meet it with your feet, your ankles, your calves, and wade in. Wade in while seeing yourself as you are: pure energy melded with the pure energy of the path.

Rise up.

"And So It Is"

Step forward.
Fall back not.
This means something.
This is instructional!
I told you this in Book One.
Step forward, and the energy of the entire universe (the All) becomes one with you.
There is nothing to fear.
There is no lack.
See from here.
Get this. And then, when you forget this, don't worry.
When you are again able, step into the river that is the All, the river that comprises everything, and live consciously from here.

Again, this is a pinnacle lesson—realizing, experiencing, and adding it to our daily practice elevates our growth into another dimension.

And the next lesson, 78, follows right on this one's heels. Each is something to be savored.

Lesson 78: Receive the Gifts of the Ethereal

And so it is ...

It is exciting, isn't it?

To those like you who are seekers, I say come here! I have much to tell you. I have much to say.

You seek and I am here.

You ask and I answer.

Fear not.

Worry not about the situations in your life or the details you ponder. Look beyond these.

Always find your center first.

Cleanse of darkness.

Fill with light.

I have attempted to explain, and it bears repeating: what seems Real to your human eyes is not.

What presents before you is but energy.

When you can grasp that you, every part of you—your fingernails, your eyes, your organs, the face you see in the mirror, the hands you work with, your being—when you can glimpse into the knowing that all is really energy, and that the pen you hold in your hand is the same, your awareness, awakening, and reconciling can deepen. Even though it makes no sense to your cerebral mind—do not try to ponder it that way.

Doubt not, for these statements are right and true, though difficult to grasp from your human position. This

"And So It Is"

is why I have continued to say, Rise up, see from here, seek from here. You will not grasp this message with your conditioned eyes. But with your new eyes, you can begin to see what is, and will remain, unseen—but is within your range of sight regardless. You see, but not fully. You comprehend, but only somewhat. Fear not. Worry not. The expansion of your mind is coming along just fine. Remember: this is a process of steps. We don't move from walking to running a marathon in one day. This takes time and practice.

To see in a new way, to remain in your center, aware of yourself and all else as energy, is a practiced skill. It will take effort and time. You are used to the illusion (it seems so real), and you have lived in it for your entire human existence. It will take time to step away and see beyond it. You will never be able to do this all the time, nor ought you try. When you drive, you still need to see the steering wheel and the road and the other cars. Nothing about the physical world you reside in is bad. You need not see the ethereal forms of things at all times. As a human, you cannot and you do not desire it. You are still incarnated on earth—enjoy the dream! Live the illusion! It is part of the reason you chose to incarnate again.

These lessons are meant to help you find more meaning and better understanding of the other side while you remain alive on earth in the vessel you call "body." They are meant to deepen your comprehension.

They are intended to let you live more connected to the All and the paradox of knowing none of it is Real. You will have more joy, depth of emotion, abundance, strength, power, light, love, radiance, connection, acceptance, and the ability to let go of anything that is not Real because you are of a different nature.

Let this happen.

Allow it to be.

Do not rush the process.

In all ways and in all moments, surrender yourself and let your soul fall gently and beautifully into the I Am, onto the canvas of the I Am.

There is no lacking in the I Am.

Receive the gifts of the ethereal while you are here on earth, and your life will astonish you.

And so it is.

"And So It Is"

Lesson 79: Choose the Life You Live

I will leave this lesson to stand on its own.

And so it is ...

As you grow, you become better able to receive, and you receive more.

As you grow, outdated belief systems gently fall away.

I make all things new.

You, life, trees, flowers: in all these things there is an ebb and a flow, a beginning and a movement forward along a continuum, a pruning or dying off of what is no longer relevant to today, and then rebirth. When I prune you, allow it to be. When you try to reach back to who you were yesterday, to how you felt yesterday, to resentments or situations from yesterday, you are reaching back to a place, a structure, an emotion, and a reality that no longer exist.

Think of it as such: When you purchase a house and tear it down, and you erect a new house on the same ground, you can no longer dwell in the torn-down structure. It is gone physically and exists only in memory. You can tap into the memory, but you cannot step into that building or reside there. The new house, the new structure, is fully operational and, likely, nicer than the one that stood before. More updated, functional, and resilient for today's needs.

Quit trying to step back into a building that is no longer there. It is gone, and just so, today you are not the person, the soul, the psyche, the physical body you were yesterday. All is renewed.

Step out.

See from the knowledge that today is a new day. And you are the decision maker as to what type of day it will be.

Is there darkness around? Yes.

You can choose that. But why? Why would you choose darkness over living awakened and as who you really are? As you reconcile with your Higher Self, your Real Self, you become aware of how often you get to choose one over the other during a single day. Light over dark. Peace over doubt. Acceptance over control and resentment. Stand in the place of choosing that which feeds you, that which is plentiful and fills your life.

Place yourself in the river even as you see that the physical world in which you live is but a temporal experience of Real. It exists, yes, but only in its expression. It is like a hologram, this earth you live in. All in it has been envisioned and created for you. When you leave the river (when you leave spirit-being and incarnate as human), you wish to again touch, hold, and feel the material things. These are not manifested as such in the ethereal world, and so, as you desire a way of knowing the physical, you and all other humans choose to incarnate.

When you are in spirit form, you are aware of human existence. After some time, all spirits desire to experience the physical world again, and they arrive on your earth as beautiful bouncing babies. When you take your first earthly breath, you forget who you really are—that you are one with All, that you are in fact divine, that you are indeed holy, part of All and pure truth, beauty, love, and energy. You

"And So It Is"

live with the belief that this identity here—your parents, your name, the house you live in, your school and your teachers—that this is who you are.

And it is ... but only in part.

Because this existence—a playground, a dreamland, a hologram—is only part of who you are. While you are on earth, embodying humanness, you cannot conceive of the All. But then you begin to awaken, to question your purpose and reason for being. Your existence is plausible, but you consider that there is more.

There *is* more, and as you slowly reconcile, access your center, and step away from the details of your life, you can find some of the answers. As I have said before, reality is not here. What you see, experience, live in, touch is all a manifestation of energy.

What is Real is behind, beneath, inside what you see with your human eyes. You can become one with this energy. You can stand in this energy and feel the connection you have to it and actually blend and meld together with it.

From here, you are on earth but accessing the Real, the river, the ethereal, the energy of the All, the light beings who are always with you—because they make up the energy that manifests into physical things. You are able to literally stand in your human vessel as energy and as one with the energy of the path below your feet, and merge together. Step into that which you call earth while seeing in this way. Create your structure, your day, your life from here. You can *choose* the type of life you wish to live while incarnated.

Have you ever changed a dream midway through the dream? Just decided it wasn't going to continue as it was?

Do that with your life.

Put yourself in this place of oneness with the energy

of the All, and change your mind to be and to have what I so want for you.

In My reality there is no lacking.

Quit seeking it for yourself.

Hold the energy in your hands.

Intend all that you desire and manifest it into your reality.

It really is that easy.

Choose wisely.

Choose not lack, fear, shadow, darkness.

Your day is yours to create.

And so it is, and all is well.

"And So It Is"

Lesson 80: Be the Light the World Needs

"Blossom, enjoy the trip, and shine brightly." This is a most beautiful lesson. I leave it, too, to stand on its own.

And so it is ...

Each time we talk, I have something to tell you.

You are coming here to be filled, to learn, and to become more.

You are excited, gobbling up my words.

Keep seeking! I am here to give.

Keep asking! I will always answer.

Fear not anything in your day—or your existence. Give more to your day, and spend less time thinking on situations, people, stuff, tomorrow. Become more present in the moment. You do not always need activity. If you must think, think on my lessons. Place yourself in the river. See that the temple is all around you. Walk with awareness, knowing that where you are, what you are doing, what you are seeing—none of it is Real. It is a temporal expression of the Real that is energy, pure energy.

When you are aware of and able to experience the moment from this place, peace washes over you. Finally, you find the exhale, and you can contemplate without consciously thinking.

You try so hard, and I tell you this: The answers you seek are not learned by effort, nor are they located through a fervent search. Allow them to simply flow to you and arrive when the time is right for you. You cannot receive them all at once.

You grow, you awaken, and you blossom as does a flower. No one expects a flower to bloom on demand—part of its beauty is in the anticipation of arrival. Then, at the right time, all qualities present simultaneously: the lingering fragrance, the bounty of color, the fullness of bloom, and the special contribution made by that moment of beauty. *You are this beauty.* You arrive as blossoms do in an ebb and flow. Each day, each moment, each time of closure and growth is a necessary part of your awakening, with the next bloom around the corner.

Stand firmly planted. Seek beauty. Seek me. Fill with light, radiate the loveliness of the All, and know that in this moment, in this breath, all is well.

We will meet again face to face in the ethereal, but while you are on earth, I want you to enjoy the trip. Don't seek the All with such force and haste that you miss your incarnation. You must awaken, and you are doing that. But as you awaken, create more, and receive the bounty and abundance I have to give, take the time to enjoy the garden of flowering blooms! Smile inside. Experience this beauty of the ethereal while you are alert and present in your earthly vessel. Your trip is short: you will again be part of the river. And as such, when you desire to incarnate again, you will go through the same stages and phases to arrive at awakening. Enjoy where you are now. Take in and savor the beautiful fragrance that is your life. As you become one with this, I can give you more and you can find greater truth, beauty, wisdom, and peace—and you can be all of those things. And then everyone around you

"And So It Is"

will also fall easily and naturally into their own place of lush beauty. This is your time, your turn.

As you see, so shall you be. And as you are, so is your life.

Be all of this truth, beauty, and sacred connection, and stand so firmly planted in it that nothing can tip you from balance and strength.

This awakening is contagious. Seek it not for anyone else but for your own soul, and as you are, as you stand, as you live, as you reside in your life, you will shine. Others want to shine too. When you are the light, you can—without effort or conscious action—light another's candle.

Be the light the world so needs.

Lesson 81: You Are Doing Just Fine

This next lesson reviews basic concepts, and we are reminded of our tasks to set our day and master the mind.

The lesson closes with "You are doing just fine."

I believe these words are a loving reminder for us to hold onto. At some point, as we continue to navigate our days and lives, we will again doubt ourselves and our progress. This reminder is here to *lift us up* on those days. Reality will continue to be as it will. "Stuff" will continue to show up. Our minds will again run amok. People, places, and things will again be difficult and challenging for us to handle. And we will go and visit yesterday, and even camp out there in our minds for far too long. Yes, to be reminded that *even when these things happen* we are doing just fine is valuable indeed.

The voice offers us this sentiment because he is so aware of what our reality on the earthly plane is like. He wants us to not feel bad when we lose our footing. When we become tipped off balance, he wants us to not feel like we've done something wrong, or haven't been connected to the river as much as we "should," or that we're losing ground in our growth. The voice tells us—repeatedly—that living these lessons does not mean that everything will become magically perfect. He does not lead us to believe that by changing our minds, by learning to see the world in a new way (as pure energy), by coming to the river as frequently as possible, we will now live a utopian existence. What he teaches is how to navigate our way through the realities of human existence and the human condition. Here he explains in yet another way: When doubt

"And So It Is"

presents, we are to claim faith. (He knows that we will face doubt again.) When fear rears its annoying head, we are to shut it down with truth. (We are human—not machines—and we will again feel fear.) When shame overcomes, we must slap it away with beauty and pure knowledge. Slap it away. We are in charge of shame, and we need never again be carried away to that dark and shadowy place inside where shame has resided in the past.

We now know what to do. We have new skills: We claim faith, shut down fear with truth, and slap shame away.

Back to the last line: "You are doing just fine."

And we are … What happens around us is not nearly as important as what we now know we are to do with it.

Yes. We are doing just fine.

And so it is …

    The day outside is as sunny as you are inside.
    If it is not sunny outside, bring your own sun to the day.
    You are light.
    You are radiance.
    When doubt presents itself, claim faith.
    When fear rears its annoying head, shut it down with truth.
    When shame overcomes, slap it away with beauty and pure knowledge.
    You are doing just fine.

Lesson 82: A New World Awaits

The voice tells us *he can teach us more* when *we live these lessons more*. That they imprint more deeply on our mind and our vessel when we lean further into and upon them. We then further awaken, and more regularly live from this awakened and aware state of being.

We are becoming, growing, deepening, strengthening, lightening, and growing in wisdom that is based in Real truth. In Book One, the voice said that we would find knowledge that is Real, true, and pure in these lessons. Not academic knowledge, but knowledge that releases our spirit—that we might fall into the deep, knowing place of "home" within us. The imprint that remains is an imprint on our soul.

The voice has often told us that the process of "becoming" takes time. Perhaps if he had begun his lessons with phrases such as the ones we are capable of grasping today, we might have found it difficult to accept or comprehend. Today, we are readily able to receive and understand these deeper concepts.

In this lesson, the way he describes our ability to cease asking about *outcomes* is something to be pondered, and savored.

That outcomes are not ours to control is made plainly in this lesson: "The planet is your river ... Let this understanding of what lives around the turn become one with you. For when you can do just that, you will be able to cease asking about outcomes. It is imperative that you get this ..."

When we become able to be one with what lives around the turn, we have no need to concern ourselves with outcomes. Our inability to see

"And So It Is"

around the turn does not mean that "what is around the turn" is not there. It means that its perfect time has not arrived. "It" (whatever outcome it is that we seek) still resides in the place of pure energy, on the edge of existence—there, but invisible to our eyes today. We are not to worry, not to stress, and not to force the ability to see or have what is not yet ours to see or have. Comprehending that what lives around the turn will become one with us in its perfect time removes the fear that the outcome we await is not coming, because we are already one with what lives around the turn; it just has not become manifest because its perfect time is not yet here. This is why we must cease asking about outcomes.

Our job is to stand united and one with the energy of the All, doing, envisioning, being, connecting, living in a way and deeply comprehending that we receive an outcome when it is realized—"it" always having resided around the turn.

It can be done.

A new world awaits ... around the turn, encapsulated in energy, and at the edges of the space we live within today. See it, know that it is there, hold it, and do what you are called to do each day in order to allow it to be realized in the material plane in its perfect time. Live from this place where you see, know—and are one with—what is possible.

And so it is ...
As you see, so shall you be.
I continue to open you to deeper truths.
When you allow my lessons to meld with your mind, your spirit, and your entire being, I can teach you more.
I give myself to you because as I heal you and teach you, you can affect those you meet on your journey.
Lean into and upon me, that I might leave my imprint

more deeply in your mind and your vessel. We are one. You are one with all you see around you and all those you encounter. Of course, not all people resonate at the same level of the soul and of their seeking. That is not a problem. Do not let them get you off kilter. Do not let them make you doubt yourself. Do not place the values and the opinions of those who are unlike you above your own. People vibrate at different levels. Do not let others affect your vision or alter your path. Your path is radiant and blessed. You must move forward with eyes up, chin up, shoulders back, lacking nothing.

When you see from your essence, and see and sense the energy of all things, I can infuse your thoughts with truth. I can show you that you are made of the very same energy as the trees, the path, the leaves, the birds that sing, and the cars that speed by. Behind the material is the Real. Behind that which presents is the All: the Real—energy, light, and truth. Let your mind go. Release yourself from mental understanding into soul understanding and allow these truths to wash over you. You and the energy behind all things are the same. You are connected.

You are oscillating at the rate of love.

And all else is doing the same.

Strip away what you see and know.

Let it all fall from your comprehension and intellect—and then *be*.

As you are, as you stand, as you live from this place, all that is in material form falls away and you meld into the All. Now you see what I mean when I say you can:

Touch the temple of heaven
Make of your life a heaven or a hell

"And So It Is"

What is all around you is *not* what you see.

What is around you is energy oscillating at the speed of what your eyes see.

Strip that away.

See from your soul.

Understand from your essence.

Let everything else fall away so you are one with the river. The planet is your river. That which you see is the river. The river is the light beings.

Everything.

The All.

It is All One: the *river*, the *light beings*—these words I have given you to describe things your human mind cannot comprehend. But it is Real, and your soul knows this to be the only real truth.

Breathe and sink into this.

Let this understanding of what lives around the turn become one with you.

For when you can do just that, you will be able to cease asking about outcomes.

It is imperative that you get this.

I healed you through my lessons of love and truth. You were enhanced, uplifted, renewed, awakened by those lessons. You can live my lessons and share them with others, that *they* might heal and awaken—that they might come to know their truth, value, worth, and purpose. And eventually they will learn that the world, their reality—their perceptions, struggles, surroundings, and the streets they walk upon—are no more Real to them than they are to you.

Then they will realize this illusion more fully and can awaken and live from their own beacon of light, truth, pure beauty, and one with the All of the All.

Igniting.

Illuminating.

Uplifting.

Awakening a new earth.

Stray not from this place. Know at all times that you live in the temple of God. You *are* the temple. The temple is everything around you and within you and of you, and as you stand united and one with the energy source of the All, I can change you and work through you. And you are empowered to erect the reality of your vision around you, as though standing before a green screen. You can see black-and-white images arising around you, pictures of sadness, despair, suffering, angst, fear, and self-doubt. Or you can create a whole new reality—a whole new world around yourself—another dimension in which to live that radiates light, pure thought, healing, connection, peaceful cohabitation, beauty, color, the fragrance of sweetness, and the singing of angelic voices. No thought of lacking can be present here.

All is abundant.

It is like Picard's home.

It can be done.

You begin; you make a start.

Then you can live from this place while seeing what is possible.

Stay close. Absorb my lessons and live from this place.

A new world awaits.

Notes

18

Apply the Knowledge of the "All"

Lesson 83: Remain Grounded

And so it is ...
    Your next level of change is upon you.
    Let go of reactive thoughts and words.
    Do not let anyone or anything influence how you are.
    Do not get swept up in the moment.
    Do not lose yourself to your chattering mind.
    Do not try to "read" another person and respond in kind.
    Be in your feet, grounded, whole, complete, and full within, in all situations. Before you speak, come to your center, the river, and speak deliberately from here. Let this place within you—this connection to the All—influence every aspect of you. Speak deliberately from this groundedness. Resonate first; speak second. Let reactive, shallow, throwaway, fill-in-the-gap conversation leave you. Now. And forever. This is a critical lesson.
    Flitting thoughts drive an empty life.
    Flitting words spread shallow thoughts.
    Ground yourself, and in every conversation you have

"And So It Is"

speak from this ground, from your core only—thoughtfully, meaningfully—and say what you mean. Then do not worry about how you are received. Your job is not to worry about outcomes. Your job is to live as I instruct.

Speak from here.

Connected.

Not everyone will like it—or you. Worry not. There is no need for them to like you when you know you are authentic and deliberate in being and speaking and acting as One.

Some people call it "the pause." It is like the pause, but it is more. This pause is to stop and speak—but from your own self.

To come to the river before you speak is to connect to the Divine and speak from there.

The voice opens this lesson with "Your next level of change is upon you." We are now ready to go deeper. In the second sentence, "Let go of reactive thoughts and words," *reactive* is the key. It is another reminder to no longer let anyone or anything else influence how we are. Another reminder to not get swept up in or consumed by the moment or by the chatter of the mind.

And then there is a new message: Do not try to "read" another person and respond in kind. *Do not "read" to respond.*

The voice is very specific in this lesson: we are to ground ourselves in every conversation, speak from our groundedness, and say what we mean. It is not for us to worry if someone likes us, wonder what they think of us, and "read" how well we are being received.

We are to ground ourselves first, and then speak and act, being both authentic and deliberate. We are not only to employ the "pause" but come to the river, connect to the Divine and speak from *there*.

"And So It Is"

Lesson 84: Bring Forth the Strength of Calm

This next lesson is another one that speaks to the conditions around us socially, politically, globally. At the time when it arrived, there was great unrest in our country. Many people were purposefully behaving in dark ways that fanned the flames of hate, becoming emboldened—even proud—to choose lies, untruths, and darkness. The voice says that darkness sometimes catalyzes more darkness, and when this lesson arrived, it most certainly felt that we were living the truth of that statement.

The voice advised, "The darkness you feel rages, stoked by many, misunderstood by more, and felt by all. Do not be consumed by this. Do not allow it to overcome you. Do not let it settle within your soul."

Instead of becoming consumed and overcome by the confusion and mind-numbing craziness, the voice reminds us to "fill," to bring forward light and to not fall into fear. When we do this and remain connected to our *strength of calm*, our energy protects us and naturally extinguishes all else.

And so it is …
    Days can be dark.
    Weeks, months, and even years, the same.

Darkness sometimes catalyzes darkness, at a primal level. It hurts. It stirs, chases, and permeates, and discomfort is awakened. Now the unrest that once calmly stirred beneath the surface ... is no longer stirring calmly.

The darkness you feel rages, stoked by many, misunderstood by more, and felt by all. Do not be consumed by this. Do not allow it to overcome you. Do not let it settle within your soul.

Surround yourself instead with peace, light, strength, confidence, and the surety of better days. Purposefully stand in your feet, grounded, eyes up, chin up, shoulders back, filled entirely with light, and step forward from here.

Bring this strength of calm with you wherever you go, that *as you are, so shall you bring. As you are, so shall you emit.* Live in this place and in this space where fear, shadow, and darkness consume you not but are extinguished by you.

"And So It Is"

Lesson 85: Perceive Your Light Beings

And so it is ...

Your earthly mind cannot comprehend everything I am asking you to absorb. Worry not. You need not understand what I am sharing as you might understand an algebra problem. This type of comprehension transcends. You cannot touch it. You cannot grasp it with your hands and hold on, but you can allow it to wash over you, knowing that your Higher Self absorbs and retains it. As you progress, you will draw upon the unseen language written on your soul. While you cannot utilize words to understand my lessons, you comprehend on the level of your soul.

When you get into the river, see and know and feel *your* light beings; they are all there to help you and support you while you are incarnated. You are the most important one of the group—not because you are "more important" but because you are the one who is on earth right now, and you have all agreed to the terms of this arrangement. The others will remain in the ethereal world as your light beings—with you at every moment and at every turn, taking care of you. Supporting, protecting, and loving you, the chosen one among your group right now, the incarnated. At another time you will remain in the ethereal realm serving as a light being to another.

There are even light beings that are so critical to your care that they will incarnate alongside you. And you will have a significant earthly relationship with this light being while it coexists in your river. *You will all have at least one of these during your time on earth.*

You may also have a painful earthly relationship with a person who is a light being to you. You might be afraid when you see them in your river. Understand that there are things you cannot or need not comprehend. Allow this to be as it is. Remain on the path, connected, gaining strength and divine nourishment from your river of light beings. And remember always: we will not lie to you or do you harm.

Breathe in. Breathe out.

By this point, the voice had added more steps to the Morning Exercise. I did not share them in Lesson 33 because we had not yet been introduced to the river, nor had we met our light beings. After we rise up and meet our higher self, he teaches us that we are to come to the river. If we like, we can wade into the river with our light beings, swim with them, ask them to comfort us, or just sit quietly in the shallows of the river's edge, residing in their presence.

When we come to our river, we are also able to see our "key" light beings—those that are most critical to our care during this incarnation. When I go to the river in the morning, I always see the same four people/beings standing at the river's edge awaiting my return. (One is my higher self—our higher selves are always one of our "key" light beings.) We can see them standing at the river's edge where they greet us and remind us of their constant presence in our lives.

In this lesson, the voice talks further about the "deal" we made with our light beings before we incarnated again: they will always be with us while remaining in the ethereal world as *our* light beings, taking care of us, supporting, protecting, and loving us. He then discusses the one (at least) light being in our river that is also in a significant relationship with us on earth—incarnated as a human being but also coexisting in the ethereal world. I know who that person is for me, and I invite you to meet your own such person at your river's edge.

The voice opened this lesson by saying: "Your earthly mind cannot comprehend everything I am asking you to absorb. Worry not." Though we cannot comprehend this knowledge intellectually, or grasp it with our hands and hold on to it, its truths remain within us at all times and our Higher Self absorbs and retains it all. When we are ready, we will come to draw upon the unseen language that has been written and imprinted on our soul.

Lesson 86: Fully Live Your Incarnation

And so it is ...

Do not push so hard.

Do not struggle so much to comprehend. I am revealing truths as simply as possible. But even so, you cannot comprehend them with your mind and see them with your human eyes.

It is when you release fully, when you let go, when you let up the anchor and dare to float along that the answers have the possibility of revealing themselves.

Worry not. This is as it is, as it will be, and as it should be.

Live your incarnation fully. Allow the glimpses of the ethereal I provide you to act as enhancement, enrichment, as opening to the Mysteries of the World. Remain open and remain one with what you have seen and experienced, but step back and firmly plant yourself in the incarnation of your earthly life. Again, you are in human form for a limited time. Do not let this time pass by while seeking only to see the place where you are not! Simply seek to open your awareness, to ground yourself more fully in that which is Real, rather than getting caught up in distraction. Let these lessons illumine, not distract. Your awakening is clearly happening. Your vessel is gaining strength, and it is becoming sleek. This is important. Yet your vessel also tires from the crossing of worlds. You must be strong

"And So It Is"

within and without. Feed your vessel healthy fuel. Move and strengthen daily.

As you see, so shall you be.

Your journey is deepening.

Now your path leads you to emit. Focus, so you emit deep, true, and calm strength.

It is not enough to be nice and kind and gentle and tender to others. It is not enough to do the next right thing. Do these, but also be and bring strength wherever you go. Lower your voice and resonate from deep within your vessel. Know that your sense of yourself, your worth, and your connection give you power. Move more deliberately. Connect more deeply. *Breathe, aware of the inhale and the exhale, and live connected at all times to the pulse of the planet.* Remain in the flow of the river of truth, one with the light beings, connected so firmly to the temple that by all appearances to the eyes of others, you are seemingly more connected to them. Know that while this is true, it is also not true.

As you strive for connection with others, connection eludes. It is an oxymoron. When you connect fully, deliberately, constantly, purposefully to the Real, to the All, to the light beings, you need not chase connection with any human; it arrives at your doorstep.

This is another reason I tell you to *never focus on outcomes.*

Live as I inspire and as I instruct, and what blossoms is the antithesis of what you believe it will be.

Today, for the whole day, focus on nothing but living from the river.

Listen for direction.

Play with the light beings in the river. Reside with them, rest with them, and be healed and nurtured and filled by them. And see everything you accomplish in your earthly plane. Feel how precise your moments are and how fulfilling is your time. Seek not productivity. Seek not precision or fulfillment. Live only from the river and your light beings, and be amazed by the depth of your contentment, your strength of purpose, and all the astonishing moments of your life.

I love you.
Trust me.
Trust in me.
Fear not. Worry not.
Live as I instruct.
Let go of outcome.
It is written.

"Do not push so hard. Do not struggle so much to comprehend."

We are to live our incarnation fully, allowing these glimpses of the ethereal that the voice provides to give us an opening to the Mysteries of the World. But as we are here in human form for such a limited time, we are to not let this time pass by while seeking only to see the place where we are not! I appreciate this reminder to not get so lost in the other side that I miss this incarnation.

In this lesson, the voice also dives further into the discussion of how we *are*, and what we emit. We have all met people who exude such deep, grounded, and calm strength that we are able to feel their connection to something greater. I met a woman like this many years ago. I was at a friend's bridal shower, and this woman was another guest. When she introduced herself to me, I immediately felt her strength and her presence. *I saw it* in her eyes. They were unwavering, calm, and grounded, and it felt to me as if she saw right through me down to my inner soul; it felt as if her highest self was looking for mine. Her eyes glistened as she smiled. I felt her calm and I felt good in her presence. *I also felt very much unlike*

"And So It Is"

her, and I have often compared myself to her, hoping to become more like her as I shed my insecurities and fears.

In a previous lesson, the voice spoke of flitting thoughts—that flitting thoughts drive an empty life and flitting words spread shallow thoughts. I think the same word applies here: flitting. Flitting eyes display lack of groundedness. I'm pretty sure I remember this woman so distinctly because she had the eyes I wanted for myself. What I didn't know then was how to get those eyes. It is not something to chase or to "achieve," because you can't have those eyes if you are not living (being) in a way that creates them. In order to have her eyes, I would need to stop flitting and become grounded. In order to resonate the same sort of strength and calm that she did, I would have to be those things inside too. So in this lesson, the voice also teaches us to, yes, be kind, and yes, do the next right thing. But we are also to *be* and to *bring* calm strength with us wherever we go.

We are to connect more deeply. To breathe, aware of the inhale and the exhale. To live connected at all times to the pulse of the planet. But not through seeking or striving, but by remaining connected to our Source.

The next lesson explains further …

APPLY THE KNOWLEDGE OF THE "ALL"

Lesson 87: Relish Each New Day

And so it is ...

A new day. Sunshine, happiness within, all seeming "right" in your world. Take it in. Relish it and cherish it, for all of you is blossoming and my lessons are made manifest.

You comprehend the river and the temple within you. You understand that you are part of the whole—your river one with the river of All. The world around you is the physical made visible. It is the illusion humanity needs in order to walk in, step through, experience life incarnated.

In the ethereal realm, the physical manifests not. But the light beings can see the physical world as you can—they are a part of it, though not in human form.

They see. And they have awaited your return to remembering who you really are so you can live, briefly during each day, between and as part of both places: the ethereal and your physical realm.

There is no need to try to understand with your mind, to force comprehension.

There is no need to try to hasten further awakening.

You need not do anything. When you come to the river, access the temple within, and live from your center, there is nothing further to do.

There is only to *be*—to simply be present here. If we have something for you to do, we will tell you. But likely all that is needed is for you to come here and reside for

"And So It Is"

awhile with your light beings. If you want to, you can play with them in the river. You can laugh, giggle, and love being together. You can let them hold you and pour their love and energy into and through you. You can let them and their divine energy become one with you. You can let them meld into you, that you will be renewed, filled, and healed, and impassioned to go forth as a more connected, light filled, confident, and radiant soul.

Or you can just sit quietly with them.

However you interact with your light beings, bring this connection to all you encounter and you will leave behind some of this love, this excess, this energy of All.

You will nearly float through the moments when you are here as a human being. Your attachment is not to the physical, yet you are more attached to the physical than ever.

Your attachment is like golden strands of light, love, of pure and true energy that guide your way and will your soul throughout the day.

Your attachment to the ethereal world while you are here in the physical realm is not Real, but it is the only Real there is.

We will nearly "float through the moments" when we are here …

However we interact with our light beings, we can bring that connection to all we encounter. The voice tells us that we will naturally leave behind some of this love, this energy of All. What a lovely way to spend the day.

Lesson 88: Step Further into Your True Self

And so it is ...

You have stepped further into your true self. The conflict that sometimes occurs is that you do not always sense this.

You will not always feel the recognition of truth. You will not always be consciously connected to the Divine or comprehend the change happening within. And in moments of unawareness, you might fall back into old thinking. You may think that if the lights are not flickering, if the sparks of the ah-hahs aren't flying, something is amiss.

This could not be further from the truth.

In truth, what is happening is that you are becoming. You are consciously living at this deeper level more regularly. You are more awakened. The ah-hahs are happening, but they are different from how they used to arrive. This is because your lifestyle, your thought patterns, your automatic responses have shifted and are naturally occurring at a higher frequency and from a different dimension of connection to the All.

So. When you think nothing is happening, you are not correct.

When you believe what is Real must always be spectacular, you are not correct.

You reside in peace more often now. You live with greater calm. You seek the simple.

"And So It Is"

You blossom radiantly and beam with all that is Real, true, pure, and beautiful.

Fear not.

All is well.

We are becoming ... We are evolving ... We are transforming.

This is a tremendous reality check, as is the next lesson ...

Lesson 89: Be the Co-Creator

And so it is ...

Calm within yourself. Calm seems the world.

At peace within yourself, same.

As you continue to renew and reenergize, you become better able to create the reality of your choosing. You know how to step into the place of co-creator. You can let go of people who are draining or even harmful to your being. You possess clarity of sight, knowing deep within that what surrounds you does not define you.

People who remain in shadow are not as able to sway you, to tilt you off balance, as they once were.

You can leave them where they are and go on your way.

You frustrate sometimes, but you can let go.

Notes

19

Three Essential Lessons

Lesson 90: You Are the Change

And so it is ...
    Seek not beyond self.
    Long for nothing.
    Never anticipate that someone else will change.
    Focus on yourself—stay here, with what you can control.
    Become, in this moment, that which you seek. Be, in this second, the energy you want.
    Bring light always.
    Do not be in fear.
    Do not aim to change the pains, the abuses, and the tragedies of the world. Do not get into the details of this, for you cannot change it—not directly.
    This is not fantasy spirit-speak I am sharing with you.
    This is not diversion.
    This is not a pivot.
    This is not bypassing emotional work.

"And So It Is"

These lessons are not to be minimized. The effort required to live them is not to be underestimated. This approach is actually harder than trying to change others and the world.

These teachings impart Real power, Real strength, and Real ability to effect change.

You can be the change you wish to see, but you cannot force others to change. You are not capable of fixing all the tragedy in the world.

When you raise *your* frequency, change *your* focus, awaken to that which is Real and place *yourself* in the middle world—the space between earth and the ethereal— you stand in Real power. And the energy and the being you become, the thoughts you transmute, truly do influence the planet upon which you live. Do not let others make you doubt or second-guess yourself, or think my approach is too simple, or that it is bypassing.

The fancy spinning of words to minimize the power of standing in, bringing, and emitting light is a meager attempt to thwart the way to real and lasting change.

Let these fly past.

Do not be influenced by anyone who alleges that these lessons are a diversion, a bypassing, spiritual flakiness, or a denial of reality.

Changing self changes the world.
Awakening within awakens a new world.
Transforming yourself transforms the world.
A new world awaits.

Those who discount and minimize the need for and critical nature of changing oneself set themselves above others, above you, and above my lessons. This serves to feed their own mind and ego and allows them to remain exactly as they are, living in judgment of all others rather than effecting real and lasting change by changing themselves. Remember: It is easier to judge another than to judge oneself. Remember: It is easier to tell someone else to change than to change oneself. Remember: If nothing changes, nothing changes.

Be the change you wish to see in the world.

"And So It Is"

Lesson 91: Rise Up

And so it is ...

Now we discuss darkness and light.

Darkness and shadow versus light.

The appeal has been made that by focusing on light, one is denying reality, bypassing emotional work, sticking one's head in the sand, and expressing spiritual flakiness.

You must all wrestle with darkness. You will become consumed by it, feel the angst of it—sometimes the terror of it—the often unrivaled anger and fear of it. You sit on the edge of the abyss, staring down into the black ink of nothingness that feels as though it is all there is. You will have this experience.

You can also choose to come out of it, and choose how you will do so. You can remain barnacled with the residue of it, or you can become free of it.

You can choose to remain in pain and shadow, or step into light and love.

The things I teach, the things I am, the things I share, are simple, logical, clean, and pure.

I give you this gift that you might once and for all be free.

Will the shadow creep up upon you yet again? Surely. But now you can see it—before it drags you to the depths of despair and into the pit of the darkest night.

You are free to be who you really are.

Clear eyes.

A fresh soul.

The depths of peace within you have touched the burning. You have not succumbed, and you have learned how to separate yourself from the fire.

Darkness is powerful, but not as powerful as light.

You will move beyond the darkness.

You will awaken, your eyes refreshed. But you will not forget the shadow.

No. This is not bypass.

No. This is not denial.

No. This is not pretending that darkness will not exist if only you don rose-colored glasses and walk barefoot through the park with daisies in your hair.

This is choosing. This is living purposefully while consciously aware of the realities of the physical world, of the physical manifestation of being human, and making a definitive decision to choose: Yes over no. Up over down. Light over darkness.

To live fully and as I inspire and instruct.

Denying not.

Pretending not.

Wrestle with the shadow; you have done so for all of your living and breathing days on earth.

If you wish to change your life, if you desire to grow beyond what you have been told you are, what you have believed about yourself—those things that keep you down, depressed, feeling unworthy, and trapped in the box you feel others have placed you in—these lessons are for you.

If you wish to rise, to create, to shine, to live anew. If you wish to live awake, in your own power, in your own glory, purposefully expressing your significant gifts. If you desire to be a candle lighting the way for others and to

"And So It Is"

radiate so brightly that you become a catalyst for change. If you want to live whole, complete, full, able to create a day of your own choosing and not one defined by that which surrounds you or by what others do or do not do.

If you seek peace.

If you want balance.

If you desire peace regardless of outer circumstances and are able—finally—to quiet the noise of the chatter in your mind …

Rise up.

Absorb these lessons.

Live as I inspire, as I instruct. Focus not on outcomes. And…

Remain separate from thoughts that dismiss the power of light, the strength of Real and pure beauty and truth.

Light, strength, beauty, and truth are here. They await you.

Lesson 92: As You Are, So Is Your Life

And so it is ...

    The river.
    The temple within.
    The middle world.
    Take your pick. None is a better name, none worse. It is the name that resonates within you that you will use. You are free to use names interchangeably as well. The middle world is perhaps descriptive for some, the river for others, the temple within for many. The choice of name is yours. But my message is one of clarity: live from this place, whichever word best fits, as consciously and deliberately as is possible.

    When we discuss distractions, we speak of those things that disrupt your ultimate focus on my lessons. Your eyes fixed on me, your mind trained on being present, in your center, living from the temple within.

    From this place you are in sync.
    From this place you are in power.
    From this place you are touching what is Real, true, and pure beauty. You are fed here: nourished, strengthened, and given the secrets of the universe.

    War will continue.
    Poverty will continue.
    People will be who they are.
    It is not your job to change the things outside yourself.

"And So It Is"

It is your job to come here and place yourself in the energy field of All, the river of the Divine, the place of being between two realities. When you are living from here, you do not directly tackle the issues of your planet and of humankind, but you do influence the waves of emotion, the direction of the wind, and the churning of the tide. *When you come here and uplift your own energy, you emit an energy unlike the wavelength of the planet.* The Source is greater than anything humans have created. The power of the All is stronger than the group of humans that has connected mentally and is emotionally committed to hanging on to the same way of being. Your people may be able to rise up; your people may not. It is still unknown.

What is clear is the need for each of you as an individual to rise up. To step forward carrying your new and enhanced energy field with you wherever you go, in whatever you do, and in all ways and times. To rise up, come to the river, the temple, the middle world and connect to the light beings—and *live from here.*

You must get this.

Do not be swayed by the illusion of those who call this spiritual bypass.

Live from this place within. Rise up. Bring yourself and your energy and the amazing light force you radiate with you wherever you go. Step forward, project this energy before you, and be in this peace. *As you are, so is your life.* You can only change what you can change: yourself.

Be the change, but be not confused about what that means.

Yes, march for a cause if you feel that is right for you. Eat a vegan diet if that calls to you. Vote, for certain. But as you consider the problems plaguing your world, if you become consumed by the darkness these situations emit, it is easy to fall into your own sense of fear, inactivity, helplessness, and hopelessness. It is easy to become tired, worn down, unable to even see where to begin. So, instead: focus. You cannot drive change on the planet by being in and of the same energy. Rise up. Step forward with strength, power, radiance, and shattering light, that the energy around you will be uplifted.

Do not discount this. Stay out of the mud. Rise up. Bring yourself to the next frequency of vibration. All too often, those who fight against the power of personal change are those who will not change themselves.

Rising up takes courage.

It takes overcoming fear.

It requires the examination of Self/Soul; the naked truth of self revealed to self; setting aside ego.

The courage to look at self.

The willingness to change self.

The dignity to stand tall even while knowing (having honestly faced) your previous habits of living in the darkness.

You must *all* reach the knowledge that you must change. Each person, each individual, each soul must face self and rise up into a new way of being, and live from the middle world, leaving ego, mind, arrogance, judgment, and selfishness at the door. You can spark change *across all of humanity* just by changing yourself within. The past falls away. The separation from the All lifts—not because you sought this but simply because it does.

The hierarchy of souls is real. Your purpose is to awaken and bring forward light and truth, carrying only what is Real. More connected to your light beings than to the events on earth. And then, ironically, you are *more* connected to the earth. It is a funny trick of the mind.

"And So It Is"

In Book One I said, "Your world is not as you think it is. That which is Real is what exists behind the material realm: the energy of all things. What you see is but a reflection—a mirage—a temporal experience of Real. Man chases what appears to matter, but nothing Real."

Chase what is really Real.

Place yourself in the river.

Do as I inspire and instruct.

Do not worry about outcomes. Do not play with outcomes. Leave them alone.

Do *your* part.

Rise up.

Today: rise up.

And stay here if you can (fall back not).

And …

That is how you change the world.

Peace.

Notes

20

You Simply Know—You Simply Are

Lesson 93: Radiate Dignity

You are accelerating, deepening, and rising simultaneously. This is your purpose, path, and destiny. Live in pain and sorrow or … light and glory. It is your choice."

And so it is …
Come to the river.
Here, your light beings rush to you.
Relax.
Feel the strength of protection surrounding you.
Here, you are renewed and refreshed.
Drink in of the light beings. Blend and merge with them. Dissolve into oneness. You, too, are the river. You, too, are a light being.
You need not do anything.

"And So It Is"

Merely be here.

Then, when you leave the river and come back to your physical reality, know that you are changed.

You are deepened, more reconciled, more attached to living as the ethereal do, and therefore you hold more power, feel deeper confidence, know greater truth. You radiate dignity, and you do not need words to explain the unexplainable.

You simply know.

You simply are.

And you do not go from here.

This depth of connection is yours. You have made another turn in the road.

Your cells relax, but they also vibrate more rapidly.

Your energy is heightened but more calm.

Your truth is revealed but unseen.

It is—because it is.

No more questioning of when, what, and how.

Utter conviction of the existence of the Real.

Utter comprehension of that which cannot be understood.

Firmly planted.

One with the All.

You are accelerating, deepening, and rising simultaneously.

Yes, step forward.

This is your purpose, path, and destiny.

When, how, and who matter not.

Live in and from this place of knowing. Doubting not. Filled. One.

Lesson 94: Live in Light and Glory

And so it is ...
>Being awake.
>Remembering who and what you really are.
>Living in the light.
>Accessing the light beings.
>Placing self in the river, the temple within, the middle world.
>All of these are fabulous. All of these represent growth. All of these mean you feel better, more powerful, more true, Real, and pure.
>But ... you are still human.
>You wrestle with darkness, with memories, with the cellular imprints of relationships that were—and can still be—hard and even damaging. Leaving behind the darkness is not bypass.
>It is choosing one's day.
>Setting one's heart on peace, light, love, my lessons, surety of path, oneness with All. All of these are important—not bypass.
>Leave the judgment of that word behind.
>When ugly and fearful feelings emerge again, wrestle them down and let them go. There is an ebb and flow to this journey. Not right, not wrong—just choosing:
>Live in pain and sorrow or ... light and glory.
>It is your choice.

"And So It Is"

Lesson 95: Share Your Spectacular Symphony

Early on, the voice inspired us to rise up into our highest selves so that we might express our beautiful gifts, that we might share our souls, our light, and our spectacular symphony with all those we encounter. He begins this final lesson with: *The symphony within you longs to be heard.*

It is your time! Let it be heard!

You have begun to realize the swell of the music and the vibrancy of the colors within. Radiate the glory of your soul's most spectacular symphony, so that as you are, as you stand, as you live, as you reside in your life, you will shine with brilliance and depth.

And so it is ...

The symphony within you longs to be heard. Share it with all you encounter that they, too, might be blessed. You have the swell of the music and the glory of the conductor at your touch; you are the one note that rises and falls as the symphony progresses; you sing along with others and you sing as a soloist. The music surrounds you and resides within.

The music is not always light and airy, or dark and ferocious. Your note rides along the musical score and remains pure and true, bounding, vibrating, and clear.

You Simply Know—You Simply Are

Your symphony is made up of the notes of the All. Your connection to everything that is, has been, and ever will be.

Never doubt the importance of the note you resonate.

Never be concerned that the note you sing or the note you play is the wrong note.

Your note is critical to the whole—as are you.

Do not think too hard on this. Do not make too much of it. Once again, this is a new way of expressing the same: *We are all one, you matter, and your note is perfect as it is.*

Allow it to become more clear, true, and resonant. No fuzz in its presentation.

It is the same with you. Vibrate brightly. Oscillate at your perfect tone. Raise your frequency to the clearest, highest, and truest resonance you are capable of.

And then, live from here.

Be from here.

Be here.

Worry about nothing else.

When you share, when you meet with others, when you give, think not of an interchange or of what you will get back. Instead, just play your note—deliver your symphony—put it out there for all to hear, to enjoy, to experience.

Give of what you have been taught so you can be of service.

Give with no expectation of receiving.

Give not to impress.

Give not to get someone to sway toward you.

Stand so solidly, reside so fully in the river that you have no need for response or accolade.

Rise up—oscillate from here, and bring forth your spectacular symphony. Give from this place. Share your music. Fulfill your purpose. Deliver your destiny.

"And So It Is"

Do not *ever* worry about outcomes: Live as I inspire and instruct. Live from the river.

Resonate your pure sound.

❖

Long after this last lesson, "Share Your Spectacular Symphony," arrived, the voice continued to use music as another beautiful metaphor. I'd like to leave you with a lesson he gave me on a recent morning walk—which is expanded upon in our next book.

Before every symphonic performance, the orchestra tunes. Anyone who has been to the symphony can recall hearing that first pure, clear, resonant "A" played by the first chair oboist to begin the tuning. The oboe was chosen as the instrument that all other instruments tune to because its penetrating sound stands out from the orchestra, so it's easy for all the musicians to hear. Its pitch is also steadier than strings, so it's a more reliable source for tuning.

We can all be as the oboe ... but I am getting ahead of the voice, again.

We are each complex beings, with the swell of symphonic music and the glory of the most magnificent conductor within. We all contribute to and form the grandest and greatest symphony of all time, and we are here with our note, and our symphony, at this time for a reason. Playing our note matters, singing our song matters, and sharing our spectacular symphony is our greatest challenge.

All orchestras tune to an "A." Most orchestras tune to a frequency of 440. Some European orchestras have, over the years, chosen to raise the frequency from 440 to as high as 450 in order to produce a brighter sound.

As you sing the song of your life, play your "note," and share your spectacular symphony that is yours alone to share, the voice invites you to pay attention. How is your note's "tone"? Is it clear and bright and able to spin effortlessly, or is it fuzzy in its presentation? How is your "A"? Is it tuned to the typical 440 or is it lower? Is it higher? Pay attention (as often as you can) to your tone, your soul, your vibration, your frequency. Depression causes us to vibrate more fuzzily and at a lower frequency. Connection to the All allows us to vibrate at a much higher frequency—even lifting us into a new dimension.

Focus on shining. Focus on clarity in your presentation. Focus on your frequency. Focus on sharing your spectacular symphony with all you encounter, that they, too, might be blessed. From this day forward: Embrace your Highest Self. Give from *this* place. Share your music. Fulfill your purpose. Deliver your destiny.

It is your turn.

If not now, when?

Notes

Closing Message from the Voice: *And So It Is, and All Is Well*

And so it is ...
    You have become stronger.
    You have come to understand what cannot be understood, see what cannot be seen with your human eyes, feel the connection to what remains hidden, and live in faith: connected to the All with no further need of proof.
    You have released into what is Real.
    For when you are one, reconciled with your Real self, nothing matters but this connection. The longing of the soul is fulfilled and the illusion of lack removed. Your eyes are stripped of what blinds them from seeing. Your feet are planted on earth. You nearly float through your day, yet are so grounded that the winds of life never tip you off balance.
    You will become stronger yet.
    You will become more fluid.
    You are strengthened in body and soul and in all ways—even your mind, and yet you have learned to set mind aside. Ego is tamed.
    You live one with the All.
    Focused on what is Real.
    Protected in the temple, the river, the middle world. You live from here: part human living, part ethereal living.

"And So It Is"

Still fully human but even more complete. A paradox all around.

Your cells vibrate more rapidly, yet they move more purposefully and in unison with a beat, a chorus not of your planet. Your comprehension has multiplied, but you still do not have words to explain or the ability to hold this knowledge.

You are infinite power and strength, and are yet to learn to tap it.

As you see, so shall you be.

Your next step is to manifest. Manifest my visions for you of abundance, beauty, truth, and power.

You have begun.

And so it is.

And all is well.

About the Author

Carleen Chase grew up in Edina, Minnesota. She currently resides in Covington, Louisiana, with her husband, their three dogs, and two cats. Carleen is a seeker, a former classical musician and corporate VP, a New Orleans–trained home chef, a loving mother and wife, and now an accidental author. Her journey of healing and discovery continues, and she and the voice are currently composing the next book in this series.

www.ingramcontent.com/pod-product-compliance
Lightning Source LLC
Chambersburg PA
CBHW051419290426
44109CB00016B/1362